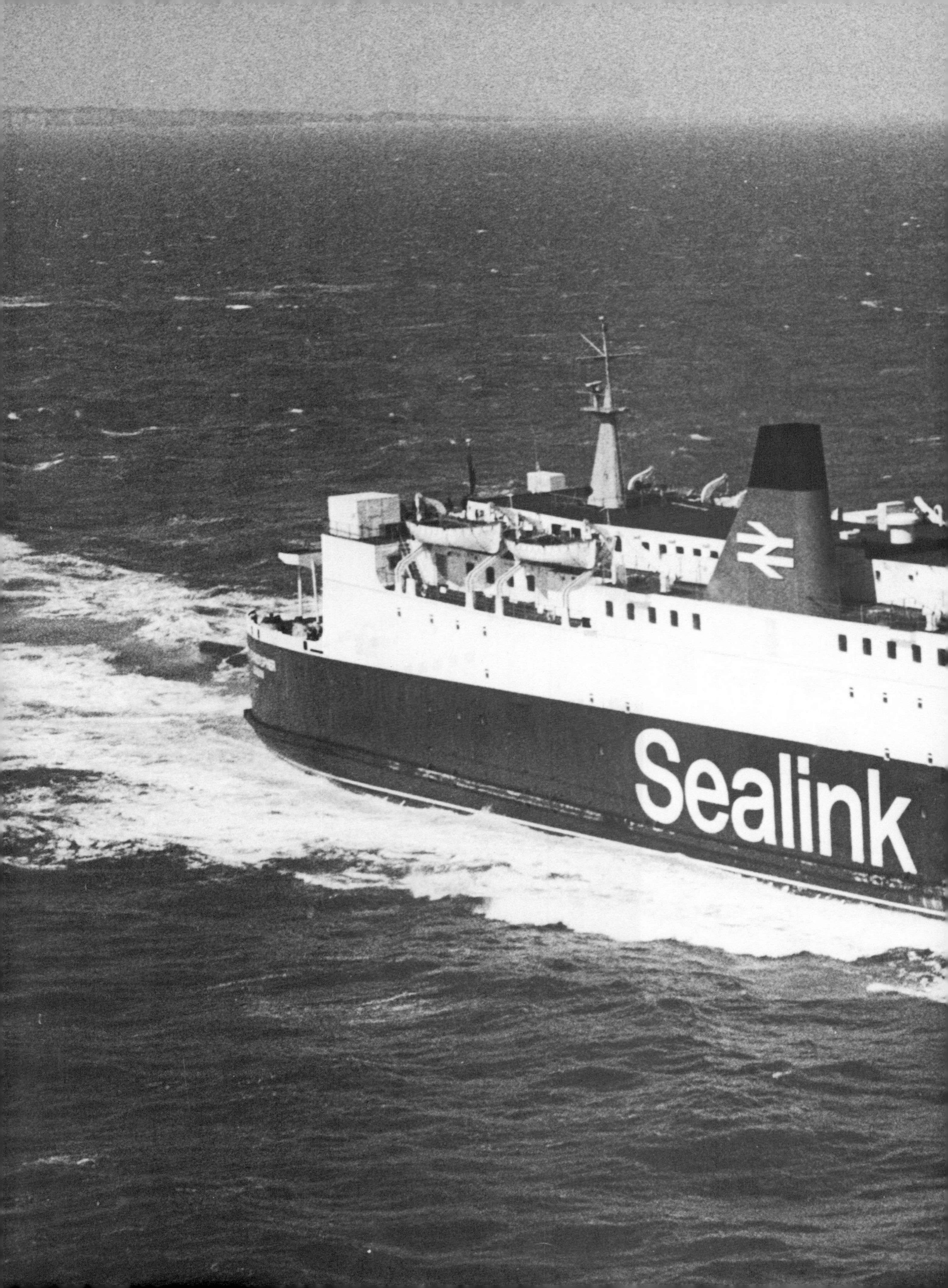
Sealink

Sealink

Brian Haresnape

LONDON

IAN ALLAN LTD

Contents

Half-title page: **The *Senlac* in Harbour at Newhaven.** *Ambrose Greenway*

Title page: **The *St Christopher*, a multi-purpose vessel of 7,003 tons; one of two new Sealink ships to enter service on the Dover-Calais route during 1981. Named after the Patron Saint of travellers, *St Christopher* can carry 1,000 passengers and 309 cars, or 62 large lorries. It cost £16million to build in Harland & Wolff's Belfast yard.** *ISR*

This page: **The *Chartres* of the SNCF/Sealink fleet in mid-Channel at full speed, showing the very distinctive shape of her funnel, in silhouette.** *Ambrose Greenway*

First published 1982

ISBN 0 7110 1209 1

Published by Ian Allan Ltd, Shepperton, Surrey; and printed by Ian Allan Printing Ltd at their works at Coombelands in Runnymede, England

Dedication:
To all the men and women of Sealink UK Ltd; with thanks.

Foreword

Foreword by
SIR PETER PARKER, MVO
Chairman
British Railways Board

Below: The *Caesarea*, of 3,992 tons, was the last cross-Channel passenger-only ferry to remain in service of Sealink UK Ltd. Built in 1960 for the Channel Islands service, she finished her Sealink days 20 years later on the Folkestone/Dover-Boulogne/Calais route. Purchased for further use, she sailed from Newhaven bound for Hong Kong on 20 December 1980. *Ambrose Greenway*

*A Journey by Design** was a landmark in the literature of railways — a stylish and visual record of their design and environment. Brian Haresnape brings the same authority, knowledge and sheer enthusiasm to this study of our shipping partners — Sealink.

Railways and their ferries were born in the same era of Victorian enterprise. They evolved and expanded together generating and satisfying the Victorian appetite for travel. Their essential interdependence underpinned more than a century of growth.

Brian Haresnape charts these origins. But like *A Journey by Design*, this book is as much of the present as it is of the past. He describes the sea change within the ferry industry during the last 20 years as it came to terms with the road vehicle. The outward shape of this challenge of change is clear enough to every passenger — larger, efficient, multi-purpose ferries with roll-on roll-off operation, modern electronic aids to navigation, and new standards of passenger comfort and entertainment. But the author also charts the organisational response to change — the creation of a separate shipping division, the development of this into an international consortium and the creation of Sealink UK as an independent subsidiary company of the Board.

And he recognises the continuing stimulus of change in the 1980s. Sealink's

* *A Journey by Design*; Brian Haresnape; Ian Allan Ltd.

competitive edge is now being sharpened as it seeks investment from the private sector. In this process of change, the rail link remains a constant — still generating some 30% of its business.

Throughout, Brian Haresnape captures the sense of excitement of an enterprise whose fortunes are linked to the sea — a sense which is in no sense lessened by the functional changes in design and modern operation.

The present competitive trading among the ferries has the Channel running red with cut throat competition. But still as the author says 'the future for Sealink looks to be a healthy one'. The past record of change and enterprise so ably recorded in this book gives great confidence for the future prosperity of the company.

Introduction :
Of Ships,
the Sea and Sealink

This is not a history book, although within its pages will be found quite a lot of history in both words and pictures. It is rather more a record of a moment in history; in the continuing saga of Sealink, whose ships and services are a familiar part of the contemporary British and Continental travel scene.

Sealink is the brand name, or trademark, of the multi-national consortium of ferry operators which operate over 10 major Continental shipping routes, as well as having various smaller operations. In this consortium is Sealink UK Ltd, the British operator and to its Continental list must be added some important domestic routes, to Ireland and the Channel Islands in particular. This book is chiefly concerned with Sealink UK Ltd, although each of the other partners features to some degree in the narrative; in particular the French connection, the SNCF (Societé Nationale des Chemins de Fer Francaise). The other partners in Sealink are the Belgian Maritime Transport Authority (RTM) and the Zeeland Steamship Company (SMZ). Together this consortium operates over 60 vessels carrying the Sealink brand name for the services involved.

Around 18 million passengers a year are carried by Sealink and in addition to the immense all- the-year-round freight transportation, some 2 million cars and 25,000 passenger coaches are carried. On certain routes there is a regular conveyance of railway wagons, giving through transit between Britain and the mainland of Europe. All this adds up to an important contribution to the transport requirements of the 1980s, and has of course a considerable influence upon the trade and prosperity of the countries involved. The tourist trade in particular has recognised a considerable asset in these ferry services, and one which it heavily promotes; nowadays with the motorist particularly in mind.

The author of this book is one of the 18 million who yearly use Sealink, and this book is the result of one man's survey of this great transport undertaking; resulting from the deep impression their ships and services have made upon me. There must be, I am sure, many people besides myself who have been similarly impressed and who would welcome an insight into the various aspects of Sealink, its ships and services, as they are presented to the traveller today. I hope this book will fill such a need.

The sea, and ships, has over the centuries created a great following

1 Sunlight glints upon a calm Channel as RTM/Sealink ferry passes a small coaster whilst at full speed on one of the busy Anglo-Belgian services which form an important part of the Sealink consortium. *Ambrose Greenway*

1

2

3

amongst men of all nations and the seafarers of today include a vast body of knowledgeable amateurs many of whom leave their weekday work to take to the sea at weekends, whenever possible. Their enthusiasm knows no bounds and in some cases their maritime knowledge and skill is quite staggering. (Sometimes alas the contrary is the case!) The present writer professes no profound knowledge, only a deep interest, or fascination. In these pages I have therefore deliberately avoided great technicality and I must apologise in advance to those specialist readers who thirst for minute detail. There are some excellent books already available (see Bibliography) and the attractive little monthly magazine *Sea Breezes* also caters extremely well for specialists' needs.

The emphasis in the second part of this book is upon the ships that serve Sealink and the background to their design. I use the word design in its broadest sense — encompassing all facets, from the original broad conception necessary to meet a need, down to the final aesthetic details which are presented to the user. To show this aspect to greatest effect I have contrasted the past and the present, with a number of pictorial sections which serve to remind the reader of the heritage and growth of Sealink.

I have heard it said, on more than one occasion, that there is no romance left in the present day ferry services, and that the ships themselves lack glamour. This I strongly dispute, and I hope this book will reveal these qualities to the reader; particularly by means of the illustrations some of which, by Ambrose Greenway, I have deliberately selected an account of their brilliant rendering of the moods of the sea and the Sealink ships that sail upon it. But perhaps this romance of the present day is of a different sort and on a different scale to that of the past, and it may be as well to define my feelings now; feelings that have developed over the years, just as one develops a taste for different foods as one grows older.

A treasured book of my childhood was the *Wonder Book of Ships*; my own copy being the 19th edition. Within its pages was a great romance, a romance of trans-Atlantic liners multi-funnelled and magnificent; of dangerous seas and icebergs; of giant shipyards; of men of a calibre apart from the man-in-the-street and of the mystique and the love of shipping. It conjured up without fail the feeling of man's uneasy but splendid liaison with the high seas. It was a book produced when the ship, and in particular the ocean-going ship, was the most

magnificent achievement of transport design and engineering of the day. At this time, on land the steam locomotive was still supreme, with such famous names as the 'Royal Scot', the 'Flying Scotsman' and the 'Cheltenham Flyer' to capture popular imagination and yet to come was the mass development of motor transport and motorways. In the skies the civil airliner, although becoming increasingly sleek and sophisticated, was as yet in its infancy as an alternative to the great liners of the seas. An alternative 'ship', the airship, showed promise in this respect until a series of disasters killed its popularity.

I read of these wonders during the dark days of World War 2, when many of the great liners depicted in my book were serving the nation as troop carriers sombre in coats of dull grey paint; or were engaged in other important wartime roles. The reality of the sea was brought home to me when my own father, a World War 1 Marconi radio operator, who had rejoined the Merchant Navy at the outbreak of war, was killed when a torpedo struck the ship in which he and other crew members were recovering from exposure, after rescue from their own ship, which had been torpedoed earlier by a German submarine.

4

This was the war of six long years which was to change the status of the ship, because of the development of the fighter aircraft and the long range heavy bomber. The skies became of steadily increasing strategic importance in World War 2 and

2 Dignity and impudence at Dieppe, with the *Senlac* coming alongside the Gare Maritime and with a typical Normandy fishing boat, *La Polletaise* in the foreground. Photographed in April 1973, when the *Senlac* was new. *British Rail*

3 Ships of the Sealink fleet carry the company symbol or logo of their owners upon the funnel, plus the brand name Sealink on the side of the hull. In the foreground of this picture, taken at Dover, is the RTM vessel the *Reine Astrid* and beyond is the solitary ALA owned vessel, the *Saint Eloi*. *Ambrose Greenway*

4 At the entrance to Dover Harbour, two Sealink ships pass in the course of their regular sailings; an everyday scene throughout the year. The *Horsa* gets under way as RTM/Sealink's *Prinses Paola* crosses the picture, in the foreground. *Ambrose Greenway*

the design of the aeroplane and the introduction of the jet engine was pushed ahead with urgency. Thus, with the return to peacetime the aeroplane assumed a far more important role in everyday transportation. The era of the 'big ships' was coming to a close; at least for passenger travel. Perhaps it was significant that the drawings that we furtively made in the backs of our school exercise books depicted as a rule aircraft in exaggerated combat or submarines, or pirates in galleons in full sail with canons firing! Never the liners of peacetime.

Although I was not aware of it at the time, during the war the gay little paddle-steamers and the coastal steamships of our holiday memories were also engaged in important work. Some were converted to hospital ships, some were used as minesweepers or like craft, and some of them were destroyed by enemy action. Not until the late 1940s was I able to journey upon the Isle of Wight ferries, for example, and in fact my first postwar voyage upon a ship of the present day Sealink fleet, was on Lake Windermere! Trips to Southampton Docks to see the latest and the last of the great liners were a special treat, and it was not surprising that the much smaller Channel steamers seemed pale by comparison.

It was the postwar recovery and increasing affluence of the British nation in the 1950s, that brought to many people, myself included, the possibility of travel abroad. No longer was a summer holiday synonymous with the pebble beaches of the south coast, the rain-soaked hills of Cumberland, or the sleepy resorts of East Anglia. Suddenly it was possible to plan an itinerary for the sun-drenched Continent at a price one could afford. Of course, many people now also experienced air travel for the first time, but a great many went by sea. At that time car ownership had nowhere near reached today's colossal scale and the 'classic' passengers (ie without a car) still predominated. The steamers were back in business!

My first taste of the open seas was on the Newhaven-Dieppe service, on board the swift and silent turbine steamer, the *Brighton*, still quite new from Wm Denny & Bros of Dumbarton. With a speed of 24kts we seemed to be truly the 'Ruler of the Waves'. I fell in love with the Channel steamers from this day on, and seized every opportunity to make journeys upon them in the years that followed. What a classic journey it was, for example, to indulge the luxury of a Pullman car from Victoria station on the 'Golden Arrow'

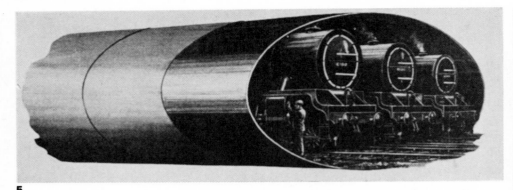

5

6

boat train and then to board the elegant steamship *Invicta* for the quick Channel crossing to Calais. Everything about this journey retained the sense of style so characteristic of prewar days; a style now of course much sought after by enthusiasts for nostalgia. It is curious that what is dismissed as old-fashioned and peremptorily discarded by one generation is subsequently seized upon by a later generation and hailed as a treasure to be preserved at all costs! Too late alas in this particular instance.*

At the time I was discovering the delights of the cross-Channel steamers, the connecting boat trains were (with the exception of some electrified Southern Region services) still hauled by steam locomotives (see table p82). The new Riddles Standard 'Britannia' Pacifics were to be found on the 'Golden Arrow' and also on the Liverpool Street-Harwich boat trains, and these and other BR steam locomotives, plus their colourful counterparts at Calais, Boulogne, etc, seemed to have an affinity with the steamships. This affinity has largely disappeared with the modernisation of the railway systems and with the replacement of the steam turbine ship by diesel-powered ferries. A journey on the footplate of a steam locomotive at speed for example, with semi-exposure to the wind and weather and with a sense of live power and movement, had much in common with the exhilaration one can experience on the open deck of a ship at sea. Today's rail travel, in air-conditioned or pressure ventilated comfort, upon smooth welded rails is matched by similar comforts on board the ferries, which

---

* Or so it seemed when I first wrote these words in 1981. As this book was going to press, news was released of a private venture which will reintroduce Pullman cars, superbly restored, between Victoria and Folkestone in 1982.

5   **Three 'Royal Scot' class steam locomotives are used to give an impression of the size of one of the huge funnels of the Cunard liner *Queen Mary*. The locomotives were the latest and greatest owned by the London Midland and Scottish Railway, when the ship was built. The artist has cleverly included a man to emphasise the scale.** *Author's Collection*

6   **A classic illustration of the way the great Trans-Atlantic liners captured the public's admiration. Here the artist has placed the Cunard steamship *Queen Mary*, fair and square across Trafalgar Square, London. Lord Nelson one suspects would have been amazed! It certainly gives a dramatic impression of the immense size of these classic ships.** *Author's Collection*

7   **Day trippers of the 1960s enjoying the sunshine and sea breezes, en route to Boulogne. For many people in the early postwar era, the cross-Channel steamers made possible their first taste of foreign shores — if only for a day!** *British Rail*

nowadays have sheltered accommodation for all passengers, although there still exists that select and hardy type of traveller who prefers the open deck, even in the roughest weather!

I write above of the 1950s. Now, 30 years or more later, the romance of the ferry services is as I have already suggested of a different aura. It is a romance built around the all-weather, all-the-year-round, intensive operation of large multi-purpose ships, offering a service to passengers and freight operators alike and giving standards of amenity parallel to those found in the competing airlines and in the larger ocean-going ships of other parts of the world.

Significantly the greatest change in the past 30 years has been brought about by the need to adapt the shipping services to suit the growth of road travel. It is the private car and the heavy lorry which have largely dictated the internal layout and specification of the latest ships to enter service. In this space of time, the various routes and services which were originally mainly rail-orientated, have also become a floating extension, or bridge, linking the motorways of each country. The rail traffic is not neglected, however, and still represents about 30% of the business.

To meet this demand for road users the ports served by the ships have had to be extensively remodelled and enlarged and the whole concept of loading and unloading vehicles has of necessity been developed to a sophisticated level which makes this once awkward manoeuvre a simple procedure. For rail passengers the connecting link between boat train and ship, once a windswept and hazardous quayside walk over inevitably wet cobblestones, and amongst cables and hawsers, is now modernised and altogether more acceptable; although bulky hand luggage still creates problems at peak times. All the associated services

8

for the motorist and rail passenger alike — the customs and passport control, information, ticket offices, etc — have been modernised to make the whole procedure as smooth as possible. On board the ships (now designated ferries) new amenities have been introduced, such as boutiques and even cinemas, to entertain the traveller, besides of course the catering facilities and bars.

However, if as I have said, the romance of today is one which exists largely because of a sense of efficiency and willingness to adapt, there are still, of course, the other elements of romance, such as the excitement of leaving a port, or sighting the shore, or watching the giant ships that cross your route in mid-Channel. There is still also of course the spectacle of the relentless sea in all its moods, to fill you with either pleasure or trepidation, and the wonderful ozone-filled air to clear the cobwebs of the mind. There is still, most basic of all, the sensation of *being at sea* and in the charge of skilled seamen. There is nothing quite like it! Even the latest aeroplane has a

plastic insulation between you and reality which makes it hard to believe you are actually flying (only the moments of take-off and landing truly capture everyone's imagination), whereas the sea constantly reminds you of your voyage through the elements; a voyage undertaken by man since time immemorial.

Underlying this sense of romance is a sense of security and of safety at sea; a sense inspired by skilled seamanship.

Safety at sea is of course of the paramount importance in Sealink's operations. The sea — beautiful in so many of its moods and aspects — is also a deadly killer, and quick to take the lives of men exposed to its mercies. The Sealink fleet has rigid standards of safety and emergency procedures which all the ships' crews are trained to observe, and in addition the ships are equipped with the most up-to-date equipment to aid safe navigation at all times. On the bridge even in port the radar sets are kept constantly warm (on stand-by) and the captain and his officers are very skilled indeed at reading the messages given by the scanners when in use at sea. Not that this has displaced the use of the 'lookout' men! Although not perched in the 'crows-nest' of sailing ship days, these men have a valuable role to play and their keen eyesight and quick reactions are an indispensable aid to navigation, in particular when many small boats are in the vicinity, and the ship encounters poor visibility.

The use of computerised electronic equipment capable of giving a radar display which describes not only the course but also the speed of ships in the vicinity is currently being added to the bridge equipment of the Sealink fleet. These compact machines can greatly reduce the risk of human error (an ever present factor in our lives) and provide a valuable 'double-check' on the observations of the lookouts and watch

9

10

8 After World War 2 the British and French Railways restored the de luxe Pullman 'Golden Arrow' service between London and Paris. New Pullman cars were built for the BR part of the journey, from Victoria to Dover, in 1951, but they retained a very prewar image of luxury. The new civil airliners presented a formidable and modern competition for this prestige trade and patronage of the train steadily declined. The Pullman car service was finally withdrawn on 30 September 1972. (The French withdrew *their* Pullmans earlier, on 31 May 1969 to be precise.) BR Standard 'Britannia' class 4-6-2 No 70004 *William Shakespeare* is seen at speed with the 'Golden Arrow', complete with British and French flags above the bufferbeam. *P. Ransome-Wallis*

9 For the short sea crossing of the 'Golden Arrow' service, the *Invicta* was normally used. Ordered for the route in 1939 she was taken over by the Admiralty and converted to an assault landing ship, and as such took part in the disastrous Dieppe raid, and the Normandy invasion. Postwar refitting, and conversion to oil-burning, plus the fitting of stabilisers made her the pride of the SR Channel fleet in the 1950s; being at that time the largest ship, capable of carrying 1,400 passengers. With a fine turn of speed, 22kts, she provided a swift and comfortable crossing. *Invicta* lasted for nearly 26 years, before being replaced by the new multi-purpose ferry *Horsa*. Her final sailing was on 8 August 1972, and she was towed to Holland for breaking-up the following month. *Skyfotos Ltd*

10 The 'Golden Arrow' train on French rails, with a Class 231E Pacific No 231E5 gathering speed as it passes Boulogne with the Calais Maritime–Paris Gare du Nord service; picture taken in July 1964. Only two Pullman cars are included in the formation, at the rear of the train. *Brian Stephenson*

11 Emergency evacuation exercise at Holyhead, with boats lowered from their gravity davits and the ship's crew undergoing drill, in lifejackets. One lifeboat still in its davits and another released from its cables nearest camera. (The ship is the *Cambria*, now withdrawn from the Sealink fleet and sold to Saudi Arabia; the owners being Orri Navigation Lines, Jeddah.) *Sealink UK*

officer on the bridge. (An odd fact of life is that most sea collisions take place in clear weather conditions, as a result of human error.)

A feature of the busiest of the Sealink routes is that they inevitably cut across the routes of deep sea shipping; because their destinations are from coast-to-coast by the most expeditious course. For example, the narrowest part of the English Channel, known as the Dover Straits, is daily the scene of some 200 vessels plying across them between Britain and Europe, and 300 more criss-crossing their path as they pass through the Straits for more distant destinations. Each day some 50 oil tankers are amongst this traffic and at least two of these will be in the giant supertanker category — over 200,000 tons (a Sealink ferry is between 5,000 and 8,000 tons). The vigilance of the Sealink crews and the efficiency of the radar equipment carried is a byword of discipline and skill which must surely rank amongst the highest traditions of seamanship anywhere in the world today.

And so to our story, which really begins

in January 1979, with the creation of the new Sealink UK Ltd company. The BR Shipping and International Services Division ended its days in 1978 with a strong trading surplus and the new company was formed upon this strong base.

Sealink UK Ltd was formed in order to give the services a firm financial framework, more in keeping with that of their competitors, who have grown in strength and numbers in recent years. The new company can be compared with them on a like-for-like basis, and with investment in new ships and terminal improvements, and with a readiness to embrace change and eliminate loss-making activities, Sealink UK Ltd is a strong and healthy Company.

Mention of the competitors serves to remind me that in 1980 a 14-year-old pooling agreement for Channel services between Sealink and Townsend Thoresen (TTF) came to an end. With P&O Normandy Ferries also plying for trade in the Channel, and with both Sealink and TTF introducing new ships, the competition since then has increased considerably and has resulted in a veritable 'price war' on these routes. The public, of course, has benefited from this, although it has caused some anxieties for the operators; and Sealink, P&O and TTF all made quite heavy losses in the recession of 1980.

Other forms of competition with Sealink's services today are the aeroplane and, on the sea, the hovercraft and jetfoil. Of the aeroplane, once regarded as the most serious threat to the future, it can now be said that it has captured its share of the traffic on the routes from Britain to Ireland and the Continent which compete with the ferries. It is unlikely to see much growth, in particular because the motorist is not so well catered for, but it remains the speediest way for business people to travel (at least whilst in the air, because

11

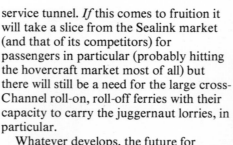

airport to city centre can be a lengthy procedure!). The hovercraft services have seen real growth, by capturing in particular the 'classic' passenger without car, who wishes to save time and money and they certainly have their role to play, although the unsatisfactory design and performance of the solitary SNCF hovercraft the *Ingenieur Jean Bertin*, has been a set-back. The jetfoil, more suited in my opinion to river journeys than to the open seas, is currently attempting to prove its worth with Sealink on an RTM service between Dover and Ostend using two craft, and initial results are said to be very successful. An earlier attempt by a company called Seajet to run between Brighton and Dieppe was abandoned; although not before the jetfoil service had made Dieppe a very popular place to visit for the day — thereby bringing new trade to Sealink in the outcome?

One further form of competition has been poised as a threat for so long now that it is in some danger of being disregarded or treated as a joke. This is, of course, the long-debated and long-awaited Channel Tunnel, linking south-east England with the northern coast of France. So many schemes and so many attempts (one or two actually physically started) have been promoted and then abandoned. But now, once again the wind blows hot for the scheme, and the finance is available provided the present British and French governments can agree on all aspects. The most likely scheme is for a single track railway tunnel, with adjacent

service tunnel. *If* this comes to fruition it will take a slice from the Sealink market (and that of its competitors) for passengers in particular (probably hitting the hovercraft market most of all) but there will still be a need for the large cross-Channel roll-on, roll-off ferries with their capacity to carry the juggernaut lorries, in particular.

Whatever develops, the future for Sealink looks to be a healthy one. At the time of writing (autumn 1981) there was a strong probability that Sealink UK Ltd was about to enter a new phase by seeking the introduction of private capital, to strengthen still further the company and to allow for future expansion. The Conservative Government's Transport Bill provides the necessary powers, and during a debate in the House of Commons on this Bill, on 22 April 1981, the Secretary of State for Transport said:

'The (British Railways) Board and the Government agree that giving Sealink access to private capital is the only sensible solution. The Board hopes that a general flotation of Sealink shares on the stock market will be possible. Obviously that is something the Government would welcome. If, on the other hand, the Board wants to decide on some other means, it is up to the Board. The one point I wish to emphasise is that the Board is in the lead, and it is for it to make proposals.'

Sir Peter Parker, Chairman of the British Railways Board has said that he sees

13

12 The railway's steamships were amongst the first in the world to use marine radar, and today's Sealink fleet carries the most up-to-date and sophisticated equipment. The revolving scanners on the mast are a characteristic of all today's fleet. *Ambrose Greenway*

13 The Racal-Decca all-weather radar display ARPA (Automatic Radar Plotting Aid) is one of the latest navigational aids to be carried by the cross-Channel ferries and it is unique in its vital 'self setting' capability. Echoes are acquired and tracked with automatic optimisation of the radar settings for each echo individually. This is a particular advantage in the 'clutter' conditions inescapable in bad weather. The captain of the *Horsa* is seen operating the ARPA, on the bridge. *Racal*

14 The Channel hovercraft services have a good share of the 'classic' passenger market and perhaps the greatest users of the hovercrafts are tourists without motor cars; once the exclusive province of the ship and the aeroplane. Both British and French Railways provide good connecting train services. Illustrated is Seaspeed's hovercraft *Princess Margaret*. Only the advent of a Channel Tunnel is likely to diminish the hovercraft's share of the passenger market because the rail passenger will have a through service from Britain to the major European cities, without change of train. *Ian Allan Library*

15 On Sunday 31 May 1981, Sealink introduced their first high-speed jetfoil service between Dover Western Docks and Ostend. Two craft work the service, the *Princesse Clementine* and the *Prinses Stephanie*, operated by RTM. By the following July, Sealink was reporting excellent results with over 15,000 passengers carried and with a crossing time of 100 minutes, compared to $3\frac{1}{2}$ hours by conventional ferry. Public response has been good, and by providing convenient connections the railways have improved the journey time from London to Brussels to $5\frac{1}{2}$ hours, city centre to city centre. Clearly the jetfoil has a role to play, but as in the case of the hovercraft, a Channel Tunnel would much reduce its appeal to the Inter-City traveller between Britain and Europe. Illustrated is the *Princess Clementine*. *British Rail*

12

14

15

clearly in this statement that the initiative lies with the BRB. Prior to this, European Ferries, the TTF owners had publicly made a bid to take over Sealink and this had rightly been referred to the Monopolies Commission. (Happily, later the Commission found in favour of Sealink and rejected the TTF bid.) Sir Peter spoke of this takeover bid when giving a Press conference on the inaugural voyage of the *MV St Christopher* on 12 May 1981. In the course of his speech, in which he welcomed the four new ships built by Harland & Wolff, he stressed that these ships gave Sealink UK Ltd new confidence for the future and would assist them in 'repelling boarders'. Here he was

16   Sealink UK Ltd's symbol of faith in the company's future has been the recent launching of four new multi-purpose ferries. Two for the Dover-Calais short sea route and two for the Irish Sea services. These impressive new ships have been very well received by the traveller. The 'Flagship' service provided since the summer of 1981 by *St Anselm* **and** *St Christopher* **was augmented in October 1981 by a new SNCF Sealink ship the** *Côte d'Azur.* **In this picture the** *St Christopher* **stands on the slipway at Harland & Wolff's Belfast yard, with a gathering of shipyard workers and Sealink guests for the naming ceremony. Bad weather prevented an actual launching until a few days later, but the** *St Christopher* **was named by BBC Television's 'Blue Peter' children's presenter, Tina Heath, and the programme has 'adopted' this ship, giving much attention and screentime to its construction and entry into service.**   *Ambrose Greenway*

referring to the 'boarding' attempt by European Ferries and he had this to say:

'. . . In our evidence to the Monopolies Commission, we have said that a take-over by European Ferries would seem to be against the public interest since it would result in major sectors of the market being dominated by one operator, and there would be areas where a monopoly would exist.

'My only other comment about the European Ferries move is to remind people that some 30% of Sealink's traffic is generated by rail, not a good fit into a concern whose philosophy has been directed towards uncomplicated ship rostering to cater for rubber wheeled traffic.

'We have made no secret of the fact that our preferred solution to getting private capital into Sealink is by issuing shares through the Stock Exchange when market conditions are right. We do not, however, as I said earlier, rule out joining forces with a commercially-suited partner as a stepping-stone to this objective.

'Whatever our final proposals, one of our primary considerations will be the maintenance of a competitive position. Our aim is to transform Sealink into a more dynamic operation than it can hope to be under the present constraints. We think buying shares in the company will be an attractive proposition, and there will be important benefits for its shareholders. For example, we know that already many

people travel with Sealink's competitors because they enjoy special fares as shareholders. With the extensive network of routes operated by Sealink UK, such arrangements would be particularly attractive to private investors.

'Our intention is to keep the company intact and to retain a substantial shareholding. This approach allows for the overriding need to safeguard the operating and commercial relationships between the company and BR, which is vitally important to the throughout rail/sea business, and pays full regard to the best interests of Sealink, its customers and the staff of both BR and Sealink.

'I am deeply aware of the strain of all this, particularly on our Sealink staff. Their staunchness in this period does great credit to them. I want them to know that the Board will be doing its utmost to ensure their future. Sealink has a great tradition and we want to make the most of it.'

I said at the beginning of this Introduction, that this is not a history book — the history is still in the making. Perhaps by the time this book is in print (and this is inevitably a quite lengthy procedure) an important new phase in Sealink's history will have begun?

Brian Haresnape FRSA NDD
Dorking, Surrey, England/Ramatuelle,
France
February 1982

Pictorial Interlude :
The Moods of the Sea

*I must go down to the sea again,
    to the lonely sea and the sky,
And all I ask is a tall ship and a star
    to steer her by,
And the wheel's kick and the wind's
    song and the white sails shaking,
And a grey mist on the sea's face and
    a grey dawn breaking.*
John Masefield—*Sea Fever*

Calm seas, wild seas; the sparkle of sunlight upon spindrift. The mysterious silence of fog; the hazy light upon a sea calm and serene. The white foam in the wake of a ferry making good speed; the pall of exhaust and the flutter of following seabirds. These and all the other moods of the sea have their own special magic.

Here, the camera of Ambrose Greenway captures to perfection some moods of the sea, and the Sealink ships that sail upon it day-in day-out, all the year round. No lengthy captions or explanations are necessary, save for the names of the ships and the routes they serve; the pictures tell their own story.

17 *Earl William* and Channel Islands sun.
Ambrose Greenway

18 A solitary seabird perches upon a rocky outcrop which oddly resembles a sleeping dog, as the *Caledonian Princess* (now withdrawn from service) silently passes, immersed in haze.
Ambrose Greenway

19 The telephoto lens emphasises the busy shipping scene in the Dover Straits as *St Anselm* crosses the paths of three cargo ships, on a choppy sea. *Ambrose Greenway*

20 Winter sea on the Larne-Stranraer service, with *Antrim Princess* taking the brunt of the headwind, but nonetheless looking magnificently capable.
Ambrose Greenway

21 RTM's *Koningin Fabiola* and in the left hand far distance another cross-Channel ferry, under lowering skies and a stiff breeze. *Ambrose Greenway*

22 *Earl Godwin* in the low raking sunlight. *Ambrose Greenway*

18

19

20

21

22

23 **A Channel Islands passenger ship.**
Ambrose Greenway

24 **The *Senlac*, sun and spindrift.**
Ambrose Greenway

25 The *Earl William* glides upon becalmed waters amidst the leisure sailors of today. *Ambrose Greenway*

26 The stately profile of *Caesarea*; now withdrawn from the Sealink Fleet. One of the last classic passenger Channel steamers of her kind, and seen here in a classic Channel setting. *Ambrose Greenway*

The Sealink UK Group

1. Sealink's Antecedents

To understand the structure and services of today's Sealink UK Ltd company, we must briefly examine its past and the changes that have taken place. If today it is the motor car and road vehicle which largely influence the design of the Sealink ships and the services they offer to the public, in early Victorian times it was the steam railway which performed this role. In fact, steam power was developed on the seas with greater rapidity than on land, and it is interesting to recall that when Stephenson's pioneer *Locomotion No 1* was trundling an uneasy course along the rails of the newly opened Stockton and Darlington Railway in order to prove its worth in 1825, the General Steam Navigation Co's steamships *Eclipse* and *Talbot* were for example, already inaugurating steam propulsion on the Newhaven-Dieppe route.

With the refinement of the steam railway locomotive, in particular by George and Robert Stephenson in the 1830s, there came the great age of railway building in Britain and on the Continent. It was a natural part of this development to build railways to serve the sea ports, and to lease the existing, or introduce new steamship services to link these ports and thereby provide a facility for through travel, for passengers, mails and merchandise. Perhaps the greatest example of this was provided by that visionary engineering genius I. K. Brunel who envisaged his giant iron steamships providing a trans-Atlantic link between the Great Western Railway and New York and North America.

Of course, in a number of instances, the shipping services had been in existence long before the coming of the railways, and they had a traffic in mails and privileged passengers, who made the overland journey by stage coach or other contrivance. In the case of the cross-Channel links between England and France, Belgium and Holland, the 'Packet-Boat' (so named, it is believed, because it carried the mail packets) was already in existence in the 17th century, serving the needs of royalty and governments, and later the wealthy landowners, by providing a regular courier service. The English diarist John Evelyn was amongst those who were privileged to travel by this means, and he records such journeys.

The new private railway companies quickly staked their interest in the existing shipping routes, in some cases buying them out completely; whilst in some other cases they instituted new and perhaps competitive services of their own. Such was the growth of the railway network that competition for traffic over roughly parallel routes became rife, and this competition extended to the sea routes. The railways won the Royal Mail traffic from the roads and this alone was of sufficient importance to make the ownership of sea routes very desirable indeed.

So it is that today's choice of routes between Britain and Ireland and the Continent, served by Sealink, mostly have their origins and growth closely linked to the fortunes of the railway companies which have fostered them over the past 150 years. As people became accustomed to travel by rail, and trade and industry prospered, so the steamship services had to be developed to keep pace. The size of ships steadily increased as the 19th century progressed, and passenger comfort and amenity was then considered to a greater degree (although by no means regarded as a necessity for the poorer classes!). Another important factor was the development of the ports, and the establishment of hotels and other amenities for the voyager.

Apart from the severe disruption to services and everyday life of World War 1, the growth and prosperity of the shipping services operated by the private railway companies underwent no fundamental change until the Railways Act of 1921. This Act provided for the amalgamation of the numerous private companies into four large groups. On 1 January 1923 there therefore came into existence the London and North Eastern Railway (LNER); the London Midland and Scottish Railway (LMSR); the Great Western Railway (GWR) and the Southern Railway (SR). The shipping fleets of the constituent companies were also taken over by these new companies; often referred to as the 'Big Four'.

Following upon the amalgamation and up to the outbreak of World War 2, further steamship development, and some rationalisation of shipping routes, took place. One important innovation, from the passengers' viewpoint, was the fitting of stabilisers — to the SR ship *Isle of Sark* in 1934 (the first in the world) nowadays regarded as indispensable. Two important aspects which grew steadily during the 1930s were the carriage of motor cars (which the SR in particular recognised as an important traffic growth), and the introduction of large train-carrying vessels. These latter vessels were already a commonplace feature in some parts of the world where islands are numerous and close together (such as Denmark) but the development of them for Anglo-Continental services was seen at the time as an alternative to the construction of the long-discussed Channel Tunnel. It was

27   The Channel Islands ferry *Earl William*. *Ambrose Greenway*

28   A notice dated 1790 advising would-be voyagers in English and French that the Prince of Wales Packet *Samuel Burton* sailed from Brighton (spelt Brighthelmston) to Dieppe every Saturday evening and from Dieppe to Brighton every Tuesday evening. *Dieppe Museum*

also a period when the cargo ship was much in demand — yet to come was the carriage by sea of heavy road vehicles and their loads.

I have already mentioned the role played by the ships of the railway fleets during World War 2; what emerged from this prolonged war was a severely depleted fleet of run-down and battered ships and run-down ports and it took some years to restore some semblance of prewar standards. New ships had to be ordered to replace aged worn-out examples, or those which had been lost completely by enemy action. It was ironically, just as progress was beginning to be made in this direction that, once again, politics intervened; this time in the form of nationalisation.

On 1 January 1948 the 'Big Four' railway companies were nationalised by the Socialist government of the day. The shipping services, together with the railways, were divided into six Regions, by geographical area. These six Regions of the newly-formed 'British Railways' (run by the Railway Executive) were broadly arranged as follows: the London Midland Region (English and Welsh portions of the LMSR; together with some outlying southern areas); the Eastern Region (southern end of the LNER in England); the North Eastern Region (northern end of the LNER in England); the Scottish Region (LNER and LMSR lines in Scotland); the Western Region (former GWR plus some LMSR and SR routes);

and the Southern Region (former SR routes). The shipping companies controlled by the four former railways also became part of BR, in certain cases transferring to another Region. Overall direction of the Railway Executive and the shipping services was in the hands of the British Transport Commission (BTC).

The marine services of the BTC, as operating in 1953 are shown in the table for the benefit of comparison with today's Sealink services. The operating region is shown. Particular note should be taken of the extensive BR operations in Scotland at this time including the Clyde fleet. Today all except the Stranraer-Larne service have ceased to be a part of BR or Sealink UK Ltd's activities.

Summary of BR Marine Services in 1953

	Region	Distance miles	Crossing Times h/min	Services
French Services				
Dover-Calais	S	21	1 20	P: Daily.
Dover-Boulogne	S	26	1 45	MP: Daily in summer
Folkestone-Calais	S	26	1 30	P: Daily. C: Thrice weekly. M: Daily in summer
Folkestone-Boulogne	S	25	1 30	P: Daily. M: Daily during summer. C: Thrice weekly
Dover-Dunkerque	S	39	4 00	F: Daily
Newhaven-Dieppe	S	64	3 30	P: Daily. MC: Daily (summer), thrice weekly (winter)
Southampton-Le Havre	S	104	7 00	P: Thrice weekly (summer), twice (winter). C: as required
Southampton-St Malo	S	151	9 00	P: Summer only. C: as required
Channel Islands Services				
Southampton-Guernsey-Jersey	S	104	6 45	P: Daily (summer), thrice weekly (winter)
	S	130	9 30	C: As required.
Weymouth-Guernsey-Jersey	S	71	5 00	P: Daily (summer), thrice weekly (winter)
	S	98	6 45	C: As required
Irish Services				
Heysham-Belfast	LM	125	7 20	PC: Daily
Holyhead-Dun Laoghaire	LM	58	3 15	PC: Daily
Holyhead-Dublin	LM	65	3 15	CL: Five times weekly
Holyhead-Greenore	LM	79		CL: Weekly
Stranraer-Larne	Sc	34	2 15	PC: Daily
Fishguard-Waterford	W	91	8 00	PCL: Thrice weekly
Fishguard-Rosslare	W	54	3 15	PC: Daily (summer), thrice weekly (winter)
Dutch and Belgian Services				
Harwich-Hook of Holland	E	116	8 00	PC: Daily
Harwich-Antwerp	E	157	14 30	C: Twice weekly
Harwich-Rotterdam	E	122		C: Twice weekly
Harwich-Zeebrugge	E	80		F: Daily
Scottish Services				
Clyde Coast	Sc			PC: Daily
Loch Lomond	Sc			P: Daily (summer)
Loch Awe	Sc			P: Daily (summer)
Lake Windermere	LM			P: Daily (summer)
Isle of Wight Services				
Portsmouth-Ryde	S	4½	0 30	P: Daily
Portsmouth-Fishbourne	S	6	0 55	PM: Daily
Lymington-Yarmouth	S	4½	0 30	PML: Daily
Ferry Services				
Hull-New Holland	E	2¾	0 30	PM: Daily
Tilbury-Gravesend	E	½	0 10	PM: Daily
Harwich-Felixstowe-Shotley	E	¼	0 10	P: Daily
Kingswear-Dartmouth	W	¼	0 10	PM:Daily
Kyle of Lochalsh-Kyleakin	Sc	¼	0 10	PM: Weekdays only

Abbreviations: C: Cargo. F: Train Ferry. L: Livestock. M: Motor cars. P: Passengers.
Services shown in italics have since been withdrawn.

30

29

31

32

Three further Transport Acts, in 1962, 1967 and 1968 further altered the structure and the operation of the regional shipping services, and abolished the BTC. Most important being the 1968 Act which created, on 1 January that year, the Shipping & International Services Division of the British Railways Board. This was to be responsible for management of the BR shipping services and also the railway-owned ports in Great Britain; whilst developing their traffic and liaising with all the Continental and Irish railway administrations, government departments and national bodies concerned with international shipping activities.

In January 1970 it was announced that the brand name of Sealink was to be adopted for the marketing of all the services, passengers and freight, operated by BR's Shipping & International Services Division, and their partners on the Continental routes. Associated with the new name was the introduction of a corporate identity programme. Two years later the first two ships to be experimentally repainted to carry the name Sealink in large letters on the sides were introduced, the *Hengist* and *Horsa*. So successful was this scheme that the following year, 1973, saw widespread application, and the brand name was firmly fixed in the public's mind. No longer were the ships and ferries of the companies involved semi-anonymous, or in no way linked visually as a joint concern; now they became instantly and constantly recognisable.

With the Sealink brandname firmly established, the formation of a new company in the United Kingdom, in January 1979, is the keystone of the arch in our story.

29 The railway-owned Port of Newhaven as it appeared, looking inland, in 1864 with two paddle steamers alongside. The railway station and hotel are in the background. *British Rail*

30 Between the two world wars the railway fleets were in the forefront of ship design and development. It was a Southern Railway ship, the turbine steamer *Isle of Sark* which was fitted with the world's first Denny-Brown ship stabiliser. The *Isle of Sark* is seen here in dry dock with the stabiliser fins visible low down on the sides of the hull. *Ian Allan Library*

31 The SR vessel *Autocarrier* built in 1931 and used to carry 120 passengers and some 30 cars between Dover and Calais. Designed as a cargo ship she was altered in form during construction, to meet the growing traffic in motorists and cars, (see also picture 43). *P. Ransome-Wallis*

32 In World War 1 the British Government developed the port of Richborough in Kent and opened a train ferry service to Dunkerque, for the transport of war equipment and personnel. Three sister ships were built specially and given the prosaic names of *Train Ferry No 1, 2* and *3* respectively. These odd-looking vessels lay idle when peace was restored, until 1924, with the Great Eastern Train Ferry Co Ltd inaugurated the first UK-Continental train-ferry service between Harwich and Zeebrugge. The LNER took over the service completely in 1934 and the three ships continued the run in their service until the outbreak of World War 2. They were then requisitioned; only No 1 survived to return to peacetime use (renamed the *Essex Ferry* and modernised). *British Rail*

33

33 The train ferry concept was demonstrated so successfully by the LNER that in October 1936 the SR and the French Railways opened their own service to Dunkerque, from Dover and three ships were built. Two were owned by the SR, the *Shepperton Ferry* and the *Hampton Ferry* and one was transferred to the ALA (Angleterre-Lorraine-Alsace, Société Anonyme de Navigation), the *Twickenham Ferry*, in 1936. They were built by Swan Hunter and Wigham Richardson Ltd. Unlike the LNER ships (that only carried goods wagons, and had no passenger accommodation) these three train ferries had a mixture of goods and passengers. Twelve sleeping cars could be carried, or 40 loaded wagons. There was also accommodation for some 25 motor cars and some lorries or motor coaches. Coal-burners, of some 2,996 tons, the ferries were requisitioned for use as minelayers and as transport ships on the Stranraer-Larne run. All three survived the war (see picture 42) and were then converted to oil-burning and restored to their normal duties. The *Shepperton Ferry* is seen here in BR colours shortly before her withdrawal and sale in September 1972. During the war she was named *HMS Shepperton*.
Ambrose Greenway

34
35

34 The 'Night Ferry' sleeping car train which was introduced between London and Paris by the SR and French Railways when the new Dover-Dunkerque train ferries commenced operation in October 1936. Passengers boarded their sleeping car at Victoria station and remained there until Paris Gare du Nord; with the entire train being shunted on to and off the train ferry at Dover and Dunkerque, as seen here. The dark blue Wagon-Lits carriages (built to suit the British loading gauge) served this route until its withdrawal on 31 October 1980. A Channel Tunnel could see the restoration of such through sleeping car trains, to destinations such as Paris, Brussels, Milan or beyond, but meanwhile a declining patronage could no longer support the running costs (and the need to build new carriages) and the service could not compete with the airlines for quick business travel. Nevertheless, in its day the 'Night Ferry' was a superb way to travel and was very popular indeed. *British Rail*

35 Before World War 2, the majority of freight carried by the railway shipping fleets was handled by cargo ships; yet to come was the container revolution (although this ship could carry 27) and the roll-on, roll-off juggernaut lorry. A typical cargo ship is seen here, the turbine steamer *Slieve Bawn (II)* built by William Denny & Bros at Dumbarton in 1936 for the London Midland and Scottish Railway, who ran her on their Holyhead-Dublin North Wall cargo and cattle service. She never had a passenger certificate. Until 1950 the ship was based at Holyhead, moving to Heysham that year and switching from one to the other for the rest of her life. In 1960 she was extensively rebuilt and converted to oil firing and in 1965 she received the new BR colours. *Slieve Bawn (II)* was sold for scrap in 1972. The cargo ship has been eclipsed by the multi-purpose ferry and the specialised container ship, in Sealink's operations.
British Rail

36

37

38

39

*War Service
1914-1918, 1939-1945*
A brief tribute to the magnificent role played by many of the ships owned by the forerunners of today's Sealink fleet, in both world wars. These sturdy vessels, conceived for peaceful purposes, and sometimes manned by the same dedicated crews that they had in peacetime, played an important and unfamiliar role in the service of the Admiralty. At a time when the passenger services were either suspended or greatly reduced, the need was for troop transport, for hospital ships and for specialised vessels of war. Some became minelayers, or target ships, some became infantry landing ships, some were used for more than one role. Some were captured by the enemy and subsequently used by them.

Destruction by mines, torpedoes, enemy action and on occasion sheer bad luck befell some of the railway steamers at war. Those that survived could tell grand story of the part that they, and their less fortunate brethren, played in those epic days of war. In World War 2, ships of the railway fleets served the Nation at the Dunkerque evacuation, and at the landings at Dieppe, Italy, Normandy and elsewhere.

36 A very effective dazzle paint scheme on the Belgian Marine Administration's new *Ville de Liege*, seen at Dover during World War 1 when this turbine steamer was used first of all as a hospital ship for the Belgian army at Calais and then as a troopship and hospital ship (as seen here) under Admiralty control. Note the extensive canvas screening disguising the promenade deck and the very effective camouflage of the bridge and forepart of the hull.
Imperial War Museum

37 Another Belgian turbine cross-Channel steamer, the *Jan Breydel*, built in 1909, had the honour of carrying the Queen of the Belgians and her children to England, when Germany invaded her country; later returning her alone to Antwerp. The ship is seen here whilst on loan to the Admiralty as a hospital ship; in dazzle paint scheme. Note the gun mounted aft and the plated-in forward end of the promenade decks, and camouflaged canvas screens.
Imperial War Museum

Sealink's Antecedents

38 The Great Western Railway's steamship *St David*, built in 1932 for the Fishguard-Rosslare service, was one of the company's ships converted for hospital use early in World War 2. She is seen here in this role during the dramatic Dunkerque (Dunkirk) evacuation, to retrieve the British Expeditionary Force as it was driven-off French soil by the advancing German Army in May 1940. In the background the sky is blackened by burning oil installations as German planes bombard the town and harbour. *St David* survived, but alas was sunk during the Italy landings of 1944. *Associated Press*

Dunkerque: 'A miracle of deliverance, achieved by valour, by perseverance, by perfect discipline, by faultless service, by resource, by skill, by unconquerable fidelity, is manifest to us all.' — *Rt Hon Winston Churchill, 4 June 1940.*

39 Another ship of the GWR fleet, the *St Julien*, built in 1925 for the Channel services from Weymouth. Converted for use as a World War 2 hospital ship (and displaying the distinctive white painted hull and the Red Cross markings that these ships of mercy carried) the *St Julien* took part in the Dunkerque evacuation, the Italy landings and the Normandy landings. On D-day plus one she struck a mine but managed to return to harbour, and with the coming of peacetime she was refitted and gave further passenger service to the GWR and to the Western Region of BR; being then scrapped in 1966. Note the barrage balloons in the sky above the harbour. *British Rail*

40 Looking every inch a 'Man o' War' in battleship grey and with guns mounted fore and aft, it is difficult to visualise this World War 2 infantry landing ship or LSI, (note the landing craft carried in large gravity davits) in its peacetime role as a cross-Channel passenger steamer! This is the Belgian twin-screw steamer *Prince Charles*, built in 1930. *Prince Charles* was converted to an LSI at the Royal Dockyard, Devonport early in the war, and served at the North African and Salerno landings, and then the Normandy invasion. With the return to peacetime this ship was destined to remain in cross-Channel passenger service until December 1960; being then the last turbine steamer in the Belgian fleet. *Imperial War Museum*

41 The LNER steamship *Vienna* introduced in 1930, seen in service as a troop-carrier, in the wartime livery of grey, with black tops to the funnels. The *Vienna* operated in this guise from her peacetime port of Harwich, and continued in use as a military leave vessel after the war, until 1960, when she was withdrawn. *British Rail*

42 After the train ferry dock at Dunkerque was destroyed during World War 2, a temporary solution to the problem of how to load railway wagons on board the train ferries was devised when services were resumed by providing a lifting gantry on the ship itself. These train ferries played an important role in delivering railway supplies and equipment during the final stages of the war in Europe. One of the train ferries is seen here, in grey wartime paint, at Southampton docks in September 1944, loading a hospital train formed of converted LNER Gresley carriages. *Ian Allan Library*

40

41

42

43

The Coming of the Car

It's an ill wind that blows nobody any good, and certainly the ill winds of World War 1 favoured the road vehicle industry. During this grim period the quantity production of cars, ambulances and lorries, and the training of men and women to drive them was a major feature of an increasingly mechanised form of warfare. After the war the roads of Britain and the Continent of Europe had a new smell — the pungent aroma of petrol fumes — upon them. Enterprising minds seized upon army surplus vehicles to develop road-haulage businesses, in competition with the railways, and the car manufacturers (blessed with new knowledge of mass-production methods) began to offer the public the cheap family motor car which gave many people their first taste of personal freedom. Motoring seized the popular taste, and has remained with us ever since, as a sort of mixed-blessing!

The sea services have witnessed the growth of the private car traffic on land, and the development of the heavy road vehicle, and have had to adapt the design of their ships and harbours to meet this 20th century phenomenon. This they have done with complete success; as is demonstrated by today's Sealink fleet.

43   The number of motorists wishing to take their car across the Channel had grown to considerable proportions by 1930 and the firm of Townsend Brothers converted a minesweeper — the *Forde* — to become a car-carrier, using this on the Dover-Calais route. To reply to this competition, the Southern Railway placed the *Autocarrier* (aptly named!) in service in 1931. This ship, built by D & W Henderson had been ordered as a cargo ship, but the design was altered during construction to provide accommodation for 120 passengers, plus stowage for approximately 30-35 cars, and suitable handling equipment. During World War 2 she was used as a troop transport (including Dunkerque) and later as a recreational ship for naval personnel. After the war she was usually based at Folkestone and had a reduced passenger capacity of 100; although mainly used as a cargo only, or cargo plus cars, ship. She was withdrawn and broken-up in 1954.
Ian Allan Library

44

MOTORING IN THE ISLE OF WIGHT. 19

Loading Motor Cars at Lymington.

No Motor Tour through England can be considered complete which does not include a run round the Isle of Wight (sixty miles). The most convenient point for crossing is at Lymington, on the South side of the charming New Forest, where the London and South Western Railway Company has provided efficient accommodation for such traffic, including slipways whereby cars can be shipped by their own power, on to specially constructed boats, thus entirely obviating the necessity of lifting, and removing a difficulty which hitherto has deterred many from visiting the lovely "Garden Isle."

The boats—towed by fast, powerful tugs—quickly negotiate the passage, which is the shortest and most sheltered, to the island. On Week-days (weather and circumstances permitting) the boats leave Lymington Town Station Wharf at 9.30, 11.30 a.m., 2.30 and 4.45 p.m. for Yarmouth, and leave Yarmouth at 8.0 a.m., 12.30, 3.15 and 5.30 p.m. for Lymington. Cars should be upon the Wharf half-an-hour before these times.
* Prior notice should be given to the Station Master at Lymington in regard to conveyance by these boats.

Special passages can be arranged on Sundays upon arrangement being made with the Station Master, Lymington (Telephone No. 7), not later than the previous day, the extra charge being £1 per Car above the ordinary rates, which are 9s. for cars not exceeding half-a-ton, and 14s. for cars above 10 cwts., including wharfage and porterage at Lymington and Yarmouth.

BANK HOLIDAYS ARE TREATED AS ORDINARY WEEK-DAYS; GOOD FRIDAY AND CHRISTMAS DAY AS SUNDAYS.

Unloading Motor Cars at Yarmouth, I. of W.

45

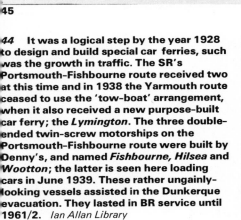

46

47

44 It was a logical step by the year 1928 to design and build special car ferries, such was the growth in traffic. The SR's Portsmouth-Fishbourne route received two at this time and in 1938 the Yarmouth route ceased to use the 'tow-boat' arrangement, when it also received a new purpose-built car ferry; the *Lymington*. The three double-ended twin-screw motorships on the Portsmouth-Fishbourne route were built by Denny's, and named *Fishbourne, Hilsea* and *Wootton*; the latter is seen here loading cars in June 1939. These rather ungainly-looking vessels assisted in the Dunkerque evacuation. They lasted in BR service until 1961/2. *Ian Allan Library*

45 Since the earliest days of motoring drivers had been able to take their prized new possessions across to the Isle of Wight usually carried on a barge towed by the paddle-steamer passenger ferry. By 1914 the demand for car-carrying to the island was sufficient for the London and South Western Railway to provide a special service from Lymington to Yarmouth, with a drive-on arrangement. The specially constructed boats were towed by fast, powerful tugs, as described in this advertisement which appeared in the LSWR timetable for 1914. *Author's Collection*

46 The BR Southern Region's first custom-built postwar car ferry, the *Lord Warden* went into service between Dover and Boulogne on 17 June 1952. With a capacity for 120 cars and 1,000 passengers, the internal layout was such that the first car on, was the first car off, by means of a turntable. The ship is seen here, dressed overall, for the initial voyage, and the first car to be driven-off, via the new ramp specially constructed at Boulogne, is carrying Mr J. Elliot, Chairman of BR and his wife and other dignitaries Used mainly on the Dover short sea and Irish routes *Lord Warden* was withdrawn in 1980 after 27 years' service, and sold to Saudi Arabia, where her new owners plan to use her to carry pilgrims to Mecca! Prior to the delivery of *Lord Warden*, the SR had operated the service with the *Dinard*, converted in 1947 to carry cars. *Ian Allan Library*

47 Although the car ferry was realised to be the ideal future vessel for the short sea routes, BR still had a very considerable 'classic' passenger business in the 1950s and early 1960s particularly on the longer sea crossings, such as to the Channel Islands (because car ownership had not reached today's colossal proportions). A limited number of cars could be carried on board the passenger ships as cargo and these were usually loaded and unloaded by crane. Here the *Caesarea* receives a car at St Peter Port, Guernsey. *Ambrose Greenway*

48

49

50

51

48 Introduction of bow and stern loading has today revolutionised the loading and unloading by means of the roll-on, roll-off procedure for road vehicles. Like the open jaw of some great fish, the *Antrim Princess* has her bow visor raised to allow the motorists to drive straight off via a short ramp. *Sealink UK*

49 The open bow doors of *St Columba* receive yet another stream of cars, via the ramp at Holyhead. The ease with which road vehicles nowadays can be loaded and unloaded means that ferries can achieve shorter turn-round times at ports, and can be more intensively worked at sea when demands are heavy. *Sealink UK*

50 The garage space on board the *Vortigern* showing the two-level parking facility, with ramps each side. This multi-purpose ferry is also able to carry railway wagons (note the tracks embedded in the decking). The upper car deck is reached by the ramps at each side of the vessel. *David Steen*

51 And the traffic still flows to and from the Isle of Wight! Making an interesting comparison with photos 44 and 45. Sealink's Lymington-Yarmouth ferry *Cuthred* releases her load of cars on to the slipway by means of the lowered ramp on the vessel itself. *Ambrose Greenway*

52

52 Nationalisation had in its first 10 years, surprisingly little effect upon the classic train and ship services, as pictured here at Weymouth Harbour in June 1959, with two WR shunting engines on the quayside, '1366' Class No 1367 and '57xx' Class No 7780, and with the *St Julian* alongside. This ship was a hospital ship during World War 2 and took part in the Dunkerque evacuation. She was also at the Cherbourg and Boulogne evacuations and then in the Mediterranean (1943) at the Anzio landings; then finally the Normandy landings. She was sold for scrap in 1961. Today's boat trains from Waterloo, diesel-hauled, still wind along the streets for the last stage of their journey and on to the quayside at Weymouth; proving quite a tourist attraction! *S. Rickard*

53 The strong link which still exists between the railways and the shipping services is well illustrated by this busy scene at Folkestone harbour, in 1959; after the electrification of the SR's Kent coast main line. In the foreground two motor luggage vans (propelled by battery power whilst on the quayside, where there is no 'live' rail), are unloading. In the background passengers from the station (on the right) are boarding the Ostend service, worked by *Roi Leopold II*; an RTM ship. Since this picture was taken the transfer facilities from train to ship, and the adjacent port buildings, have all been completely modernised. *British Rail*

54 In 1970 two ships, the *Hengist* and the *Horsa*, appeared with the brand name Sealink painted in large white letters on the blue sides of the hull. This was adopted for all the British Sealink ships the following year, and this style has been widely copied by Sealink's partners and competitors, and contemporaries elsewhere. Here the busy Channel scene is well portrayed with the *Horsa* crossing another ferry. *Ambrose Greenway*

53

54

Pictorial Interlude : Steam Trains and Steam Ships — The End of an Era

Through Queen Victoria's long reign and on into the first decades of the 20th century, the growth of the steam railway, and the steamship sea routes, was a major contribution to the trade and social intercourse of Britain and her European neighbours. The steam locomotives became steadily more powerful and the trains they hauled became faster and more comfortable. On the seas, the steamships were refined in design and steadily increased in capacity and comfort. The link between lands, by iron wheel up iron rail, and iron ship upon the seas, was forged by steam. The 'classic' days of steam-powered travel are briefly recalled here. The coming of the aeroplane and the motor car has changed the pattern of

travel to a considerable extent, but both the railways and the sea services still flourish — albeit adapted in form and in motive power to meet the needs of today.

55   A painting by Howard Geach, c1865, showing 'The Boat Train, South Eastern Railway, Dover Harbour'. Note hand–flag signalman on extreme left, as the train is hauled off the then completed portion of the Admiralty Pier in rough weather. The SER train ran to London (Charing Cross) via Redhill. In the lefthand background the train of the London Chatham & Dover Railway can be seen, departing for Victoria station, London. *Bucknall Collection*

56   The Victorians were not loathe to experiment, and in 1874 the Thames Ironworks built the *Castalia*, for a new

company called the English Channel Steamship Company. This vessel consisted of two half–hulls with a pair of paddle wheels in tandem between them. This artist's impression gives a very accurate idea of her form and decoration. Four funnels were carried, and she must have looked very impressive at 'full steam ahead'! A second freak ship called the *Bessemer* appeared the following year, and this had a swinging saloon on the single hull, intended to minimise the seasickness experienced on a rolling ship. Neither of these ships was a success, but a third 'freak' appeared in 1877. This was the *Calais-Douvres*, and this catamaran proved sufficiently successful (if somewhat slow) to be taken over by the London Chatham & Dover Railway and operated on the Channel for nine years; finally ending her days as a coal hulk on the Thames. (See the next illustration). *Ambrose Greenway Collection*

55

56

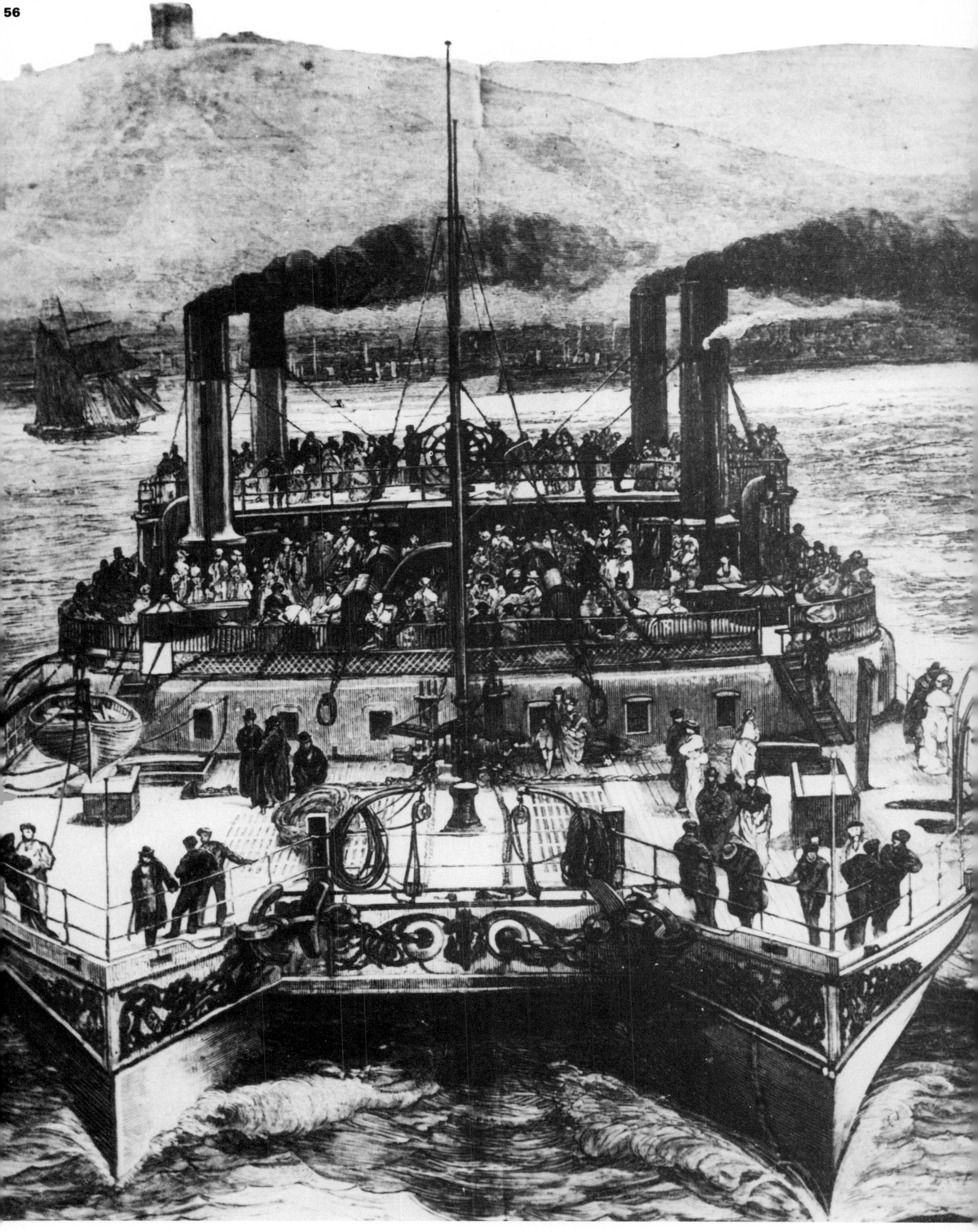

57

58

57 Admiralty Pier Dover, about 1886/7, with a London Chatham & Dover Railway train headed by an 0-4-2T and with the paddle-steamer *Maid of Kent* alongside. This ship was built in 1861 by Samuda for the Jenkins & Churchward fleet, and was taken over by the LCDR in 1864. In the lefthand background can be seen (over the parapet) three of the four funnels of the double-hulled ship *Calais-Douvres*, built by Leslie of Hebburn in 1878, and operated by the LCDR for nine years (see previous illustration). *J. W. Sutton*

58 The Gare Maritime at Dieppe, with two railway steamers alongside, and the connecting boat train for Paris about to depart, hauled by an elegant 4-6-0 of the Chemin de Fer Ouest-Etat. The departure of the boat train was evidently a popular public spectacle to judge from the crowd of onlookers in the foreground! *Ian Allan Library*

59 The Gare Maritime at Calais, with the paddle steamer *Dover* alongside. The *Dover*

59

60

was built in 1895 by Denny Bros for the LCDR, one of two new ships (the other was the *Calais*) ordered for the Dover-Calais night service. (A third was soon ordered, the *Lord Warden* of 1896.) Progress in marine design proceeded at such a pace however that these three nice ships were destined to be the last paddlesteamers built for the Calais service and all three were disposed of after only 15 years service, in 1911. On the quayside a Northern Railway of France 'Atlantic' locomotive shunts a brakevan in front of the impressive station building; since destroyed by the ravages of war. *Ambrose Greenway Collection*

60 The paddlesteamer *Duchess of York*, built by Lairds of Birkenhead for the South

Eastern Railway in 1898, and used on the Boulogne run; where she is seen in the inner harbour of Boulogne. Placed in reserve when the technical breakthrough of the turbine steamers made the paddlesteamers somewhat outclassed, she worked excursion traffic and stand-in duties. In 1910 she was sold to S. Lambrus-chini Ltd of Buenos Aires and renamed *Rio Uruguay*; being used on the Plate estuary service to Montevideo and eventually broken-up in 1930. *Ambrose Greenway Collection*

61 The introduction of the turbine steamships with their increased size and mechanical efficiency did not herald the end of the grace and elegance of the Channel

steamer. The rake of the funnels and masts, and the lines of the hull, combine to give the turbine steamship *Victoria*, for example, a most pleasing appearance. She was built in 1907 for the South Eastern & Chatham managing committee, by William Denny & Son, and served on the short sea routes until 1928 when she was bought by the Isle of Man Steam Packet Co and converted to oil-firing (in 1932) for their Heysham service. On 21 December 1940 she hit a mine off the Mersey Bar lightvessel, but was repaired and altered to become an infantry landing vessel. Released by the Admiralty in 1946 this grand old ship served a further 10 years on the Isle of Man route before being broken up at Barrow in January 1957. *Ambrose Greenway Collection*

61

62

63
64

62 The close spacing of the two raked funnels on the steamship *Reindeer* gave her a very businesslike air. Built in 1897 for the Great Western Railway's Weymouth-Channel Islands service, the *Reindeer* is seen here approaching St Peter Port Guernsey, at speed. A brief spell on the Fishguard-Rosslare run in 1914 was brought to a halt when she was requisitioned for conversion to an auxiliary minesweeper in 1914. She served in the Mediterranean, in the Gallipoli campaign, being returned to the GWR in 1919. Refitted as a passenger ship at Southampton she worked excursions and stand-in duties to Guernsey; she was sold for scrap in November 1928.
Ambrose Greenway Collection

63 The London and South Western Railway Co's steamship, the *Caesarea*, built in 1910, one of a pair (the other being named the *Sarnia*). These turbine steamers were built by Cammell Laird & Co at Birkenhead, for Channel Islands service. Of modern appearance for their time, with a single funnel, they were triple screw ships and had an accommodation for 980 passengers in two classes. The *Caesarea* gave brief war service in 1914/1915 as an armed boarding vessel, but then continued her normal run. In 1932 she was sold to the Isle of Man Steam Packet Co and renamed *Manx Maid*; she was converted to oil-firing by her new owners and used on the Liverpool service. With the outbreak of World War 2 the ship was again requisitioned and became a fleet messenger vessel and then a troopship. Renamed *HMS Bruce* in 1941 she then served as a Fleet Air Arm tender from 1942 to 1946. After return to her owners (minus main mast) she ended her long career as a weekend excursion ship and was finally broken-up in November 1950. *Ambrose Greenway Collection*

64 The elegant turbine steamship *Canterbury* of the prewar SR fleet; photographed at Dover. The ship was built by Denny's in 1928 for the new London-Paris 'Golden Arrow' rail and sea service which had been introduced in May 1927. With a gross tonnage of 2,912 when new, the accommodation was first class only, and very luxurious indeed. In 1931/32 second class accommodation was added (due to the effects of the Depression) and her gross tonnage increased to 3,071. World War 2 saw her used as a transport (including Dunkerque) and then as a Fleet Air Arm target ship. In July 1941 she was sent to work the Stranraer-Larne run, and then the next year withdrawn for conversion to a troop landing ship, taking part in the Normandy invasion. Final Admiralty service as a military leave ship saw her released and refitted for the restored 'Golden Arrow' service — starting on 15 April 1946. However the new *Invicta* replaced her on this prestige run the same year and the final 16 years of this attractive vessel's career were spent on the seasonal Folkestone-Boulogne service; being sold for scrap in Belgium in 1965.
Ambrose Greenway

Farewell to the 'classic' steamers

Just as the railways of Europe and elsewhere have seen the transition from the faithful steam locomotive — glorious in its style and manner but modest in its overall efficiency, when compared to the diesels and electrics that have replaced it — so the Sealink fleet has seen the passing of the 'classic' steamship, in recent times, and with it the era of the passenger-only vessel. Two steamships still served the fleet until the autumn of 1981, the *Maid of Kent* and the *Caledonian Princess*, but these were passenger and vehicle ferries in layout. They could perhaps be regarded as the 'grand old ladies of the fleet', and now they too have gone.

Some of the more recently retired steamships are shown here as a brief pictorial souvenir of some of the last of a long line; and the picturesque little paddle-steamers are not forgotten! They too had a magic appeal of their own. Happily some of these ships have found new owners, as described in the captions.
Adieu Vapeur!

65 Steam whistle of *St Patrick* in full cry!
Ambrose Greenway

66 The turbine steamship *St Andrew*, built by Cammell Laird & Co at Birkenhead in 1932 for the Fishguard and Rosslare Harbours Co, with four Parson's turbines and oil-fired boilers and a speed of 21kts. She, and her sister ship *St David* were managed by the GWR. Wartime service included use as a hospital ship at Dunkerque (rescuing several hundred sick and wounded men) and with the cessation of hostilities *St Andrew* reopened the Fishguard-Rosslare service. She is seen here in latterday condition, in January 1965 when the initials FR were added in white to the red funnel with black top, when she was under the management of the Western Region of BR. This 3,035ton steamer was finally withdrawn in the summer of 1967.
British Rail

65

66

67

67   Heading smokily into the dusk on 1 December 1973, the paddle steamer *Wingfield Castle* is seen en route for New Holland, working on the Humber Ferry service. One of the trio of paddle steamers, the *Lincoln Castle*, *Wingfield Castle* and *Tattershall Castle* which plied the 20-minute crossing between Hull and New Holland, until replaced by the diesel-driven paddle boat *Farringford* see photo 101. The *Tattershall Castle* was the first to be withdrawn in 1972, bought by a Newcastle company. The *Wingfield Castle* was bought by Brighton Marina in 1974. The *Tattershall Castle* was the first paddle steamer in the world to be fitted with radar, by BR in 1953.

All three of these attractive ships were coal fired, and one man stoked and fed the boiler with up to 7 tons of coal each day.   *A. Eaton*

68   The paddle steamer *Lincoln Castle*, built in 1940, heads into a snow storm, as it leaves New Holland pier, also on 1 December 1973, on the Humber ferry service. The *Lincoln Castle* lingered-on in service to become Sealink's last coal-fired ship, being run in conjunction with the *Farringford*. The *Lincoln Castle* failed a boiler test in 1979 and was offered for sale by Sealink. Now the ship is owned by Mr Francis Daly, whose plan to berth her in Princes Dock, Hull for use as a floating

restaurant was opposed by Hull City Council in the summer of 1979.

The Humber ferry was closed when the new Humber road bridge opened in 1981 but in its postwar heyday it carried some 75,000 passengers, 100,000 cars, 12,000 vans and 150,000 parcels on about 11,000 crossings each year.   *A. Eaton*

69   A poignant reminder of the days of steam. The stokehole of the *Lincoln Castle*, with Assistant Engineman Bill Rheman busily feeding coal to the firebox. Temperature could reach up to 120 degrees in this confined space.   *Sealink UK*

68   **69**

70

70   Working in reverse, the paddles of the pretty little steamer *Ryde* set the water in a flurry of action. The *Ryde* was the last 'classic' paddle-steamer ordered by the SR for its Isle of Wight service in 1936, and delivered the following year by William Denny & Bros Ltd, of Dumbarton. Used on the Portsmouth-Ryde service, this coal-fired steamer was requisitioned by the Admiralty for war service as a paddle-minesweeper, and later she was converted to an anti-aircraft vessel, for Thames defence. She took part in the Normandy D-day landings, as an anti-aircraft ship at Omaha beach and was awarded the Battle Honour 'NORMANDY 1944' for this action. The 566ton *Ryde* was the first SR ship to be reconditioned after the war and she continued on the regular run until two new diesel ships the *Brading* and *Southsea* were introduced in 1948. Mainly on stand-by and relief work after that she remained long enough to be repainted in the new BR colours in 1965; being withdrawn due to high running costs in 1969. (By then she had made more than 50,000 crossings on the Portsmouth-Ryde route.) The last 'classic' paddle-steamer to remain on the South Coast, *Ryde* was sold to a company operating a marina on the river Medina near Newport IOW and renamed *Ryde Queen*, being used as a nightclub. Damaged by fire in 1977 she has been repaired after purchase by new owners.
Ambrose Greenway

71   The *Maid of Orleans* had the double distinction of being the last of the long line of ships built by Denny's of Dumbarton for the Dover Straits, and of being the first ship launched by the BTC after nationalisation, on 17 September 1948. She was actually ordered by the Southern Railway, to replace the ship of the same name sunk during the war. This good-looking steamer had a gross tonnage of 3,776 and a top service speed of 22kts. Her fastest-ever Channel crossing was just 58 minutes from Dover to Calais. The distinctive shape of the funnel, like a 'fireman's helmet' was a modification made in 1958/9 to combat problems with exhaust fumes polluting the ship. The *Maid of Orleans* ended her days as a one class only ship (originally there was two-class accommodation) working the former 'Golden Arrow' schedule to Calais. A scheme was considered for converting her to a side-loading car ferry for use on the Fishguard-Rosslare route but nothing came of this. Her last season in service was the summer of 1975, and then — being increasingly costly to run — she was laid-up at Newhaven and sold for scrap in Spain that November. The *Maid of Orleans* is seen leaving Dover in the twilight of her career.
Ambrose Greenway

71

72

72   Two 'classic' steamships, the
St Patrick and the *Côte d'Azur* seen at
Folkestone. The *St Patrick* (left) was built in
1948, originally for the Fishguard-Rosslare
service operated by BR's Western Region.
This 3,147ton passenger and cargo vessel
was transferred to the Weymouth-Channel
Islands service in 1959. Then from 1963-
1965 she worked on the now closed
Southampton-St Malo route; finally going
to Folkestone for the Boulogne run on
which she finished her Sealink days in
1971. She was sold to a Greek shipping firm
for further use as a Mediterranean ferry and
renamed the *Thermopylae*; running
between Italy and Greece. Not a success,
she was sold again and the new owners
Agapitos Bros, renamed her *Agapitos 1*, and
ran her for two years between Piraeus and
the Cyklades Islands of Syros, Tenos and
Mykonos. She was replaced by *Apollon*
(ex-*Lisieux*) and laid-up to rust away at
Perama.
    The rakish-looking *Côte d'Azur* (right),
one of the most attractive of the postwar
Channel fleet, was built for the SNCF at Le
Havre in 1950 specifically for the Calais-
Folkestone service. Her narrow stream-
lined Valensi funnel was a most distinctive
feature. Withdrawn in September 1972 she
was sold the next year to a firm based in
Monaco. Plans to use her (renamed briefly
Azur and then *Marie F*) on a service to
Sardinia, and possibly Corsica, did not
materialise. Nor did a plan to use her as a
floating Casino, and she was laid-up near
Marseilles until she was towed away for
scrap in southern Spain in 1974.
Ambrose Greenway

73   Resting at Newhaven; the *Normannia*
and behind, the *Lord Warden*. The
Normannia can be seen with a sizeable dent
in her bows, which caused delay in
obtaining a seaworthiness certificate prior
to sailing to a Spanish breaker's yard in
November 1978. The white line added to
her funnel was in preparation for sale to the
Dubai firm of Red Sea Ferries, for use as a
pilgrimage ship; a deal not concluded. The
Normannia, of 3,543 tons when new, was
built in 1952 by Denny's for the
Southampton-Le Havre overnight service,
with two-class accommodation for about
1,400, including 325 berths. With the
closure of the route imminent, *Normannia*
was converted to a car-ferry, on Tyneside,
in 1964, with a capacity for 111 cars and
500 passengers; the gross tonnage was
reduced to 2,217. She operated the Dover-
Boulogne run, also from Newhaven
occasionally and stood-in for the *Holyhead
Ferry I* for the inauguration of the
Holyhead-Dun Laoghaire car ferry service,
when the new ship was delayed. Based
mainly at Dover in its later years the ship
was loaned to the SNCF Calais-Dover
service for six months in 1973 and then
spent some time on the Weymouth-
Channel Islands run. Her final claim to fame
before being put up for sale was the
inauguration of the new service between
Dover and Dunkerque West. The *Lord
Warden* (in the background) is described in
more detail on page 85. Following sale by
Sealink in 1980 she became the *Al Zaher*,
owned by the Babond Trading & Shipping
Agency and registered at Jeddah.
Ambrose Greenway

73

74

74 The *Duke of Rothesay* was one of the three sister ships built in 1956; this one by Denny's of Dumbarton. She was put on the Heysham-Belfast service, with first and second class accommodation for 1,800 passengers (600 first class, including 240 berths). Gross tonnage was 4,780 and a number of cars could be carried as cargo. She was converted from a 'classic' passenger ship to a car ferry in 1967 but was still restricted as a vehicle carrier because of her deck height limitations. From 1967 to 1971 she was used on the Fishguard-Rosslare service, as a side-loading car ferry. Then followed a long period laid-up before she was used again on the Holyhead-Dun Laoghaire and Heysham-Belfast routes. She made her last trip on the latter route in March 1975. She was broken-up on the Clyde. Her sisters were sold in 1975 and have survived in new ownership. The *Duke of Lancaster* is owned by Empire Wise Ltd of Liverpool and used as an accommodation vessel; berthed in 1980 at Llanerch-Y-Mor, Deeside. The *Duke of Argyll* was sold to the Greek shipping line Corinthian Navigation Company, based at Limassol, Cyprus and is now named the *Neptunia*. These three steamships were amongst the most handsome of the postwar railway fleet. *Ambrose Greenway*

75 The *Avalon* was conceived as a 'mini-liner' with a standard of accommodation which allowed her to be used as a cruise ship at off-peak times. The *Avalon*, sold in November 1980 to the Seafaith Navigation Ltd of Nicosia, Cyprus and then later to India for scrapping was the largest ship ever owned by the railway fleet when it first appeared. Of 6,584 gross tons, this elegant 'classic' turbine steamer was built in 1963 by Alexander Stephen & Sons Ltd, Linthouse, specifically for the night service on Harwich-Hook of Holland route. She had accommodation for 750 passengers, with 331 first class and 287 second class berths, plus 132 'un-berthed'. For cruising this was reduced to 300–320 one class. The cruises were to places as far afield as Copenhagen and Tangier, Lisbon and Oporto, Gibraltar and Santander. With the entry into service of the *St George* she was released for more cruises and then the decision was taken to convert her to a car ferry as seen in this picture, with the gross tonnage reduced to 5,142. In this form she could carry 1,200 passengers and 198 cars. Her final route was the Holyhead-Dun Laoghaire service in company with *St Columba*, and the arrival of the new *St David* has allowed her to be withdrawn. *Ambrose Greenway*

75

76

76 Farewell! The last sailing of the *Caesarea* in Sealink service on 4 October 1980. The Dover lifeboat and an RAF rescue helicopter keep her passengers entertained, on a special charter crossing from Folkestone to Boulogne in aid of the RNLI. The *Caesarea* and her sister ship *Sarnia* were custom-built for the Weymouth-Channel Islands service, with one-class accommodation for up to 1,400 passengers, in considerable comfort. Everyone was assured of a seat, and space for their luggage, and these ships became very popular, giving a boost to the route's receipts. Designed for both day and night crossings, 25 double and 12 single cabins were provided, whilst for 400 or so passengers there were aircraft-type reclining seats in sheltered accommodation on the open decks; the rest of the seating being in the lounges, etc. The *Caesarea* was built in the East Cowes yard of J. Samuel White in 1960 and *Sarnia* followed in 1961. The introduction of a new roll-on, roll-off service to Jersey in 1973 using the *Falaise*, began the decline in the usefulness of these two fine ships on the Channel Islands route, as they could not carry many cars, by comparison. *Caesarea* was moved to Dover in February 1976 and spent the next five seasons on the short sea routes, where she became very popular. After withdrawal she was laid-up at Newhaven until sold in December 1980 to Superluck Enterprises SA, and she sailed for Hong Kong as the Panamanian *Aesarea* that month.
Ambrose Greenway

77 The *Earl Leofric*, formerly *Holyhead Ferry I* was built at Hebburn in 1965 for service between Holyhead and Dun Laoghaire. In 1973 the ship was switched to the Dover route, but returned to Holyhead for the 1974 and 1975 seasons. In 1976 the ship underwent major alterations at North Shields, returning to service fitted with a bow visor to make her a through loader. This increased her car capacity from 150 to 205. The name was changed to *Earl Leofric* and the modernised ship again took up service on the Dover short sea routes. The coming of the new *St Anselm* displaced her and she was laid-up at Newhaven in December 1980. After only 16 years in service the ship was sold for scrap to a Northern Spanish shipbreaker. The fuel

costs of the very thirsty steam turbines was the major factor in the decision to withdraw her. Her gross tonnage when new was 3,879. *Ambrose Greenway*

78 The *Maid of Kent,* 3,920 tons, was the last steamship in the Sealink fleet. She performed her final sailing on Friday 2 October 1981, on the Weymouth-Cherbourg route, a seasonal service which closed the same day for the winter. The *Maid of Kent* (Sealink's only vessel registered at Dover) was built by Wm Denny & Bros in 1959 for the Dover-Boulogne car ferry service, and she marked the commencement of a new BTC design philosophy for passenger comfort and

amenity. The *Maid of Kent* had room for 190 cars and 1,000 one-class passengers. Cars were loaded and unloaded at the stern. In 1974 a new Sealink route was introduced between Weymouth and Cherbourg (seasonal) and the *Maid of Kent* operated on this from the opening until her withdrawal seven years later. She was used a couple of times after her official withdrawal on 2 October 1981, as a relief ship to the Channel Islands when *Earl William* was off the service; her sale had not been finalised at the time of writing this book. Many enthusiasts considered her to be the best looking of the car ferries. With her passing we mark the end of an era.
Ambrose Greenway

77

78

2. The Sealink UK Group Today

The British partner in the Sealink consortium, Sealink UK Ltd, has within its own company structure a number of subsidiary companies. These range from two associated shipping services, the ALA (SA De Navigation Angleterre Lorraine Alsace) and Sealink Isle of Man or Manx Line (Holdings) Ltd, to land-based activities related to the services, such as Sealink (Scotland) Ltd, Sealink Travel Ltd and the Fishguard and Rosslare Railways and Harbours Co; and also to concerns

such as Passro (Shipping) Co Ltd, and Passtruck (Shipping) Co Ltd.

The head office is located in Eversholt House, London, close by Euston Station, in a building once known as the Railway Clearing House headquarters. Under the Managing Director Mr L. C. Merryweather, there are: managers, concerned with planning, personnel, traffic, sales, ports and catering; Chief Superintendents for marine and engineering; a naval architect; officers for

finance and public affairs; plus of course the financial accountant and company secretary.

The traffic management of the shipping business is divided into two main sectors: (a) Continental and Channel Islands and (b) Irish, Isle of Wight, Isle of Man and

79 A striking view of the *St Columba,* dressed overall for her entry into service on the Holyhead–Dun Laoghaire route in **1977.** *Tony Bentley*

79

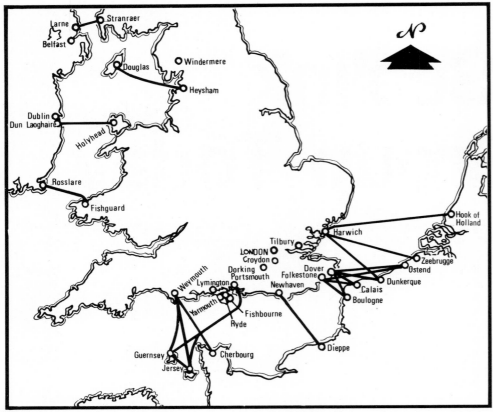

80

81

The 10 ports in the UK which Sealink UK Ltd either owns, or uses, each has a manager. For Parkeston Quay, Harwich, Newhaven, Fishguard, Holyhead, Heysham and Stranraer there is a Shipping and Port Manager; for Dover a Shipping Services Manager, for Weymouth a Shipping Manager; for Folkestone a Port Manager and for Portsmouth a Manager — Channel Islands Services.

The Continental countries served, and the Channel Islands, Northern Ireland, Republic of Ireland, Isle of Man, and the Isle of Wight, all have Sealink offices. In Belgium these offices are located at Ostend and Zeebrugge, in France at Boulogne, Calais, Cherbourg, Dieppe and Dunkerque and in Holland at the Hook of Holland. The Channel Islands offices are at Guernsey and Jersey, with English offices at Southampton and Portsmouth. In Northern Ireland there is an office at Belfast and another (run by Sealink Scotland Ltd) at Larne. Eire has two offices, one in Dublin and one at Rosslare; the Isle of Man has one in Douglas and one in the UK at Preston; the Isle of Wight one at Portsmouth, and Sealink (Scotland) Ltd has its own office in Glasgow. The lake services on Windermere are now under the control of the Shipping and Port Manager at Heysham, but there is also an office at Windermere. It can be seen from this that Sealink UK Ltd is no remote London-

Estuarial services. Each sector is controlled by a chief traffic manager and separate management teams are responsible for the profitable development of the individual routes. Scotland has its own manager, located at Glasgow for Sealink (Scotland) Ltd. Every Monday morning a managerial conference is held at Eversholt House, to review services, problems, finance, etc, and to keep a wary eye upon the operations of their competitors!

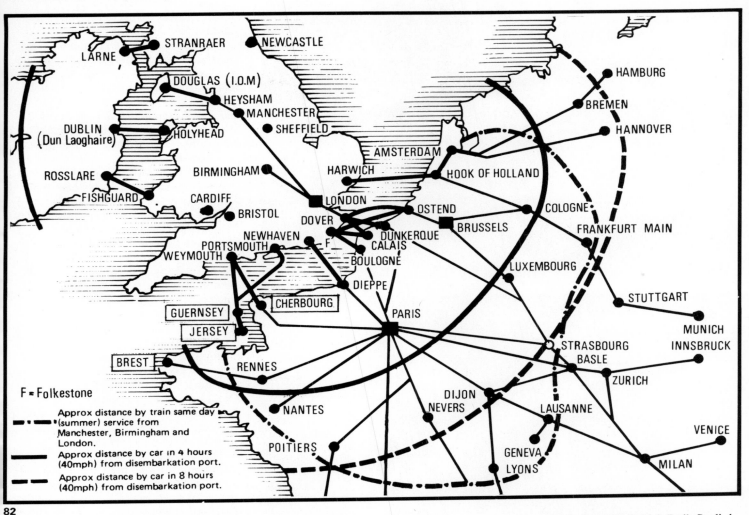

F = Folkestone

—·—·— Approx distance by train same day (summer) service from Manchester, Birmingham and London.

———— Approx distance by car in 4 hours (40mph) from disembarkation port.

– – – – Approx distance by car in 8 hours (40mph) from disembarkation port.

82

based concern, operating with its 'head in the clouds'; it is very much on the ground and in constant contact with all aspects of its services. The map reproduced shows the location of all the main Sealink activities, and includes the London head office and the International Traffic and Accounting Centres at Croydon and Dorking.

For the travelling public and the trader, the facilities for information, bookings, etc are being steadily improved, with new

80 This map shows the location of Sealink UK Ltd ports and offices, including the Croydon and Dorking International Traffic and Accounting Centres, the Tilbury-Gravesend and Humber estuarial ferry services and the Lake Windermere 'Freshwater' service.

81 The new £2½ million Sealink travel centre at London's Victoria station, showing the service positions; all linked to a central computer to facilitate instant booking of vehicle space and passenger accommodation on boat trains and ships. *Sealink UK*

82 The service to the tourist, showing Sealink routes and first day holiday destinations — the distances a traveller can reach by car and train on the first day of a holiday.

telephone answering services which provide up-to-date recorded details of all Sealink sailings 24 hours a day. New and modernised Travel and Car Ferry Centres are an important feature in sales promotion. At London's Victoria station for example, in April 1981 a £2½ million centre was officially opened, adjacent to Platform 2, which provides a single location to concentrate all Sealink's selling services. The modern style office has 16 service positions which provide for advance reservations and ticket issues; a ticket office with seven positions for: 'day of travel' reservations, a 'jetfoil' check-in facility and information desk, waiting lounge, toilets and a bureau de change office. There is also a baggage registration hall.

An additional feature of the Victoria centre is a Holiday shop with six service positions for the sale of car ferry and Continental Motorail tickets and Sealink Travel Ltd inclusive tour holidays. Instant booking of vehicle space, passenger accommodation on ships and BR boat train reservations are made possible by a computer linked to each service position and feeding to a master computer. For travel agents many extra telephone lines have been installed to deal with their reservation requests through the new computer system.

In association with British Rail, Sealink is well represented in home and overseas sales offices, and these too are being modernised and improved. In Paris, for example, the BR office is located in the heart of the City on the Boulevard de la Madeleine and handles over-the-counter business totalling approximately FF2million a year. BR and Sealink also liaise with the Continental railway systems and operate joint sales offices at important locations. The traveller arriving by SNCF at the Marseille St Charles station for example in the summer of 1981, was greeted by an eye-catching display including a scale model and large coloured diagram of Sealink's latest flagships. North America is also well informed on BR and Sealink facilities, by means of travel offices and advertising.

It could be said that there are two distinct facets to Sealink's business. One is the all-the-year round carriage of freight, road vehicles and a certain number of classic passengers and motorists; the latter greatly increased in the summer by the tourist category of passenger. The other is the off-peak carriage, deliberately promoted, of excursionists, day-trippers and package holiday travellers, and we will look first at this.

To fill ships at off-peak times of the year (when they will in any case be sailing,

83

84

French Riviera, Italy, Greece and other sun-drenched resorts, or perhaps to Holland, Germany, Switzerland or Austria, there is a trend for the French, for example, to head for England, Scotland and Ireland — thereby happily creating a two-way flow in the holiday peaks. (See map of first day distances.) The biggest single factor in this tourist trade is the phenomenal growth in private car ownership over the past quarter of a century. The motorist of today frequently chooses to take his car on holiday, although perhaps using the railway car-carrying services 'Motorail' for the longest stretch. Many people own or hire caravans to tow behind their car, and the motor-caravan is enjoying a new popularity because of its self-contained freedom. Camping on sites with good amenities is on a scale never before experienced, and to some degree it has affected the trade of the classic resort hotels and guest houses. The ferries carry a large share of this tourist trade, including that of the motor-coach operators, with their package tours. Development of the roll-on, roll-off loading principle has enabled Sealink to cope with this ever-increasing demand with the minimum of terminal delay.

The 'classic' passenger, perhaps a businessperson who prefers not to fly, or simply a person who finds the ferry service most convenient, is by no means neglected and considerable improvement

83 The tourist trade is a major (but seasonal) element in Sealink UK Ltd's operations, and both the private motorist and the coach traveller now boards the ship with the minimum of delay, via the roll-on, roll-off loading ramps installed at the ports; illustrated is Boulogne. *Ambrose Greenway*

84 The 'Motorail' service (first introduced by BR) has given a wide range of car-carrying routes to the motorist in Britain and on the Continent, and these are linked-up to the car ferry sailings to provide good overall timings. The passengers have the comfort of the train for the long distance journey whilst their car is conveyed on a special wagon, attached to the same train. Pictured here is the Boulogne-Milan service at the loading point in the Gare Maritime at Boulogne. Upon arrival, the motorist fresh and relaxed simply collects his car ready for use in the holiday area of his choice. *British Rail*

85 The comfort and efficiency of the rail services connecting the Sealink shipping routes with the major centres of Britain and Europe continues to be a major asset in marketing the advantages of this combined mode of travel. British Rail have modernised the rolling stock used for the connecting boat train services from the Channel ports, in recent months, and these electric trains offer a new, brighter, standard of passenger comfort; in keeping with that to be found on the Sealink ships. Depicted here is one of the Class 411 refurbished electric trains. *British Rail*

but with fewer passengers) an imaginative range of special offers are widely advertised, and these include the motorist with car in many instances. In addition special cruises are arranged, and one of the most imaginative of these is the 'Jazz ship' to Jersey, which has now been run in the month of March for five years in a row.

This 'Jazz ship' weekend excursion covers travel from Portsmouth to Jersey, full board accommodation for three days (two nights) at the Jersey Holiday Village and coach transfers. Throughout the weekend a famous Jazz Band plays on board ship and at concerts on shore. Also included is a Sealink duty-free bonus pack containing a litre bottle of whisky or gin and two litres of wine. (All for £52 per person in 1981).

I quote the 'Jazz ship' as an example which has become justifiably popular, but there are many more, to cater for many tastes. These range from one day to

several and include 'Cordon Bleu cookery courses' in Dieppe, visits to famous beauty spots with coach travel included and mini-cruises including one on the Cunard luxury liner Queen Elizabeth 2 to France (Cherbourg), with a Sealink ship providing the return trip. There are numerous package mini-holidays and weekends with hotel rooms included in the price and also longer Continental bargain stays. This vigorous marketing of the Sealink ships in off-peak periods, as well as providing some wonderfully cheap holidays, serves to promote the image of Sealink in the public's mind throughout the year, and to keep fully active ferry staff who would otherwise be underdeployed, or even perhaps redundant.

The tourist trade has become a major aspect of the ferry services with the steady growth in the numbers of people choosing to holiday abroad. For example, whilst the British tend to head south to Spain, the

has been made to the rail services most often used by these passengers between ports and cities. A very large traffic in students of all nations, using special cheap travel facilities, is a major portion of the 'classic' trade of today. On BR the Southern Region's express electric trains that operate the boat train services between London and the Channel ports are currently being modernised at Swindon works and attractively refurbished. On the SNCF, the carriages used for the Calais, Boulogne and Dieppe-Paris services now consist of the latest 'Corail' stock, which is air-conditioned and superbly smooth riding. The French also utilise their gas-turbine trains for some connecting services and these are both fast and comfortable. The Dutch, the Belgians and the Irish railway systems have all improved their boat trains in recent years. Most important has been the development of greatly improved rail and port terminal facilities and the rail passenger of today enjoys facilities which stand comparison with those offered by the competing airlines. For the longer sea journeys, to Ireland and Holland in particular, excellent cabin facilities allow a good night's sleep on board ship, whilst some connecting trains consist of sleeping cars or couchettes or both, for the overnight journey by rail. These latter include some of the 'Motorail' services, where the motorist can sleep whilst the car is carried to his chosen destination; usually in the same train formation.

The roll-on, roll-off, or 'ro-ro' development has particularly benefited the road haulier. An important feature from Sealink's viewpoint is that this traffic is all-the-year round, and also in many instances, overnight. This gives a good utilisation of the ferries at times when the tourist trade is at its lowest. Sealink makes

Traffic Figures Sealink UK Ltd 1980

	Passengers	*Accompanied* *vehicles*
Continental routes	8,160,000	940,000
Irish routes	2,470,000	370,000
Channel Islands	890,000	98,000
Isle of Wight	4,970,000	590,000
Estuarial Services	1,780,000	60,000
Total	18,270,000	2,058,000

FREIGHT

	Lorries/ *Trailers*	*New import/* *export vehicles*	*Containers*
Continental routes	250,000	140,000	78,000
Irish routes	200,000	24,000	60,000
Channel Islands	20,000	10,000	—
Isle of Wight & Humber Ferry	90,000	—	—

On the three Continental Train Ferry routes 49,000 loaded rail wagons were conveyed in 1980.

a point of offering good comfort and amenities to the lorry drivers whilst their vehicles are on board, and it is significant that, for example, many Spanish drivers heading for the UK, with perhaps fresh fruit or similar produce, deliberately choose the Dieppe-Newhaven service because it offers comfort and relaxation en route, although it is a longer journey time.

Two other aspects of the freight business are of considerable importance. One is the carriage of new cars, lorries, caravans and vehicle chassis (a two-way traffic of export and import) and the other is the growing use of containers. The export and import road vehicle traffic is again all-the-year-round and by siting vehicle parks adjacent to the ports, the manufacturers can deliver their new cars and lorries at their will, to be placed under a security patrol in these parks. The ferries can usefully fill vacant places on the car decks at off-peak times, with this traffic.

The container has revolutionised the door-to-door carriage business, by allowing a trader or manufacturer to transport his wares overseas, in a custom's-sealed container without the need to load or unload en route, from one form of conveyance to another — always a moment of high risk for loss or breakage. The road-hauled container is paralleled today by the railways of Britain

and Europe, that provide special wagons to carry containers in fast freight trains. On BR the 'Freightliner' business has built up an excellent UK network and these services are linked to Sealink which itself operates container ships.

Last, but by no means least, there is the freight traffic that reaches Sealink by rail. Until quite recently it seemed that this was in some danger of being eclipsed by the juggernaut lorry and the container traffic, but the introduction of fast modern air-braked rail wagons including specialised types for the conveyance of important industrial products in bulk (and capable of running on the tracks of both BR and the Continental rail networks) has led to an increase of this traffic. Recently, the introduction of large bogie wagons, of German design, has brought greater carriage capacity and flexibility of loading, at attractive rates for the through journey. The specialised ships that carry the rail wagons, and in some cases lorries as well, are well utilised throughout the year, and plans exist to introduce two new 'Jumbo' train ferries, with more than double the present capacity, specifically for the North Sea routes. Instead of the present 26 maximum wagon load they would each carry 104 wagons per voyage. New terminal facilities at Harwich would be required for these 'Jumbo' ferries. One factor influencing the resurgence of the rail wagon business is the steadily increasing cost of road vehicle fuel. However, if the long-awaited Channel Tunnel (or bridge) materialises, this is traffic which would probably be largely lost by Sealink, as it would make the entire journey by rail.

To give the reader some idea of what Sealink UK Ltd carries in a year, in passengers and freight, I give above the 1980 figures (a year actually somewhat adversely affected by a recession in the British economy).

86
87

88

89

90

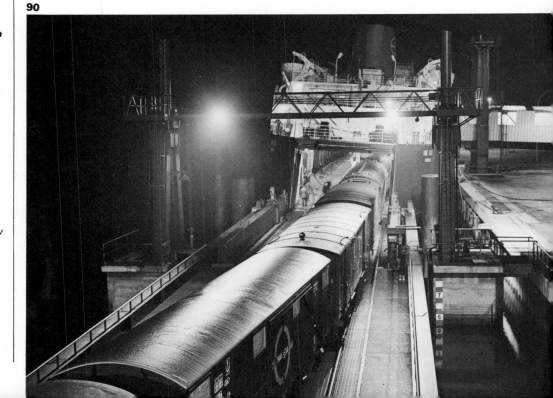

86 The European railway network linked to the ships of Sealink via the ports, has benefited from consistent technical improvement since the last war (after which much of it had to be virtually rebuilt — such was the degree of destruction it suffered). The French railways — SNCF — have recently introduced extremely smart and comfortable new carriages on its boat train services. These are known as the 'Corail' stock; fully air-conditioned and superbly quiet and smooth-riding. A Paris-Calais Maritime boat train, hauled by a BB electric locomotive is seen here (formed of the new 'Corail' stock) standing at Amiens in September 1979. *Richard Capper*

87 A very typical present-day scene at Dover, with in the foreground a mixture of private cars towing caravans, solo cars, juggernaut lorries, and new vehicles (in this instance Land-Rovers and Range-Rovers) for export. All await their call for loading. Two ships are seen, the *Vortigern* nearest the camera, and RTM Sealink's *Roi Baudouin* behind. The ugly concrete structures at the top of the picture are known as the 'Pens'. Too small for submarines, they were used by motor torpedo boats in World War 2.
Ambrose Greenway

88 It's winter; it's nighttime. Not many passengers to be found, but Sealink nevertheless does a flourishing trade, in the conveyance of new cars for export, and loaded railway wagons on Anglo-Continental runs. This scene was photographed on board the *Suffolk Ferry*; now withdrawn and replaced by the larger *Speedlink Vanguard.* *Sealink UK*

89 The carriage of freight in containers has been one of the most remarkable areas of business growth in recent years. British Rail have encouraged the use of road/rail containers by developing the 'Freightliner' network and this is linked to Sealink's container ship service at Harwich Parkeston Quay. The special container loading gantry is seen here, with *Sea Freightliner II* alongside. *Ambrose Greenway*

90 The Sealink/ALA multi-purpose ferry *Saint Eloi* receives a trainload of wagons by night. Nearest the picture is a *Transfesa* wagon, originating from Spain and used to transport fresh fruit and vegetables to Britain. *Transfesa* have their own rail-connected depot at Paddock Wood, Kent from which they despatch the produce by road to the markets and shops of Britain. *British Rail*

3. A Survey of the Routes

SEA ROUTES: EUROPEAN

Harwich-Hook of Holland (Multi-purpose services)
Crossing time: 6hr 30min (day service), 8hr 30min (night service)
Frequency: Two sailings each way daily (one day and one night daily throughout the year) with additional services during peak periods
Motorail services: There are numerous services from Brussels and s'Hertogenbosch (approx 2hr from Hook of Holland). Car sleeper services from Hook of Holland to Poznan during July and August only

Harwich-Zeebrugge (Containers)
Crossing time: 8hr

Frequency: Seven crossings each way per week

Harwich-Zeebrugge/Dunkerque (Train Ferries)
Crossing time: 7hr (to Zeebrugge)
Frequency: Up to three each way daily

Dover-Dunkerque (Multi-purpose)
Crossing time: 2hr 20min
Frequency: Up to six sailings each way daily

Dover/Folkestone-Ostend (Multi-purpose)
DOVER-OSTEND (by ship)
Crossing time: 3hr 20min to 3hr 50min
Frequency: Up to 15 sailings each way daily — up to eight car ferry sailings from

Eastern Docks; up to three car ferry sailings from Western Docks; up to three passenger only sailings from Admiralty Pier

DOVER-OSTEND (by Jetfoil)
Crossing time: 1hr 40min
Frequency: Up to six crossings each way daily

FOLKESTONE-OSTEND
Crossing time: 4hr 15min
Frequency: Up to three sailings each way daily

Dover/Folkestone-Calais/Boulogne (Multi-purpose)
DOVER-CALAIS
Crossing time: 1hr 30min

91

Frequency: Up to 12 sailings each way daily
Connecting car sleeper services to: Nice, Mulhouse

DOVER-BOULOGNE
Crossing time: 1hr 45min

92

Frequency: Up to five sailings each way daily from 23 May 1982
Connecting car sleeper services to: Avignon, Milan, Narbonne, Biarritz, Frejus/St Raphael

FOLKESTONE-CALAIS
Crossing time: 1hr 50min
Frequency: Up to three sailings each way daily
Connecting car sleeper services to: Nice, Mulhouse

FOLKESTONE-BOULOGNE
Crossing time: 1hr 50min
Frequency: Up to three sailings each way daily
Connecting car sleeper services to: Avignon, Milan, Narbonne, Biarritz, Frejus/St Raphael

91 *Princess Paola,* 4,356 tons; RTM/ Sealink fleet for short sea routes.
Ambrose Greenway

92 Bustle and breeze in the Channel, with SNCF/Sealink's *Chantilly* on the left, Sealink UK's steamship *Earl Leofric* on the right (this ship has now been withdrawn) and framed between them one of Townsend Thoresen's ships. In 1981 Sealink introduced two new multi-purpose ferries to the Dover-Calais service, followed by the new SNCF ferry, the *Côte d'Azur.*
Ambrose Greenway

Newhaven-Dieppe (Multi-purpose)
Crossing time: 4hr
Frequency: Up to six sailings each way daily

Weymouth-Cherbourg
Crossing time: 3hr 55min (2 April-1 October 1982)
Frequency: Up to two sailings each way daily

SEA ROUTES: IRELAND
Holyhead-Dun Laoghaire (Multi-purpose)
Crossing time: 3hr 30min
Frequency: Basically two each way daily, but some extras at peak periods

Holyhead-Belfast/Dublin (Containers)
Crossing time: 4hr 30min (to Dublin)
Frequency: One each way daily

Fishguard-Rosslare (Multi-purpose)
Crossing time: 3hr 40min
Frequency: Two each way daily except Mondays, off-peak (Peak: July/August)

Stranraer-Larne (Multi-purpose managed by Sealink (Scotland) Ltd)
Crossing time: 2hr 15min
Frequency: Up to nine sailings each way daily (1981 statistics)

Sealink

93

94

93 The 4,018ton *Earl Godwin*, for Channel Islands services. *Ambrose Greenway*

94 The 5,590ton *Horsa*; short sea routes. *Ambrose Greenway*

95 The 761ton *Cenwulf*; Isle of Wight car ferry service. *Ambrose Greenway*

95

SEA ROUTES: CHANNEL ISLANDS
Weymouth-Channel Islands (Multi-purpose)
Crossing times: Weymouth-Guernsey 4hr 30min. Weymouth-Jersey 7-8hr
Frequency: Up to two sailings each way daily

Portsmouth-Channel Islands (Multi-purpose)
Crossing times: Portsmouth-Guernsey 7hr. Portsmouth-Jersey 9hr 20min
Frequency: One service each way daily

SEA ROUTES: ISLE OF MAN
Heysham-Douglas (Multi-purpose operated by Sealink Isle of Man (Manx Line Holdings))
Crossing time: 4hr (day sailing), 6hr 15min (night sailing)
Frequency: One each way, with extra sailings May to October

SEA ROUTES: ISLE OF WIGHT
Portsmouth/Lymington-Isle of Wight (Passenger service-Ryde. Multi-purpose-Yarmouth and Fishbourne
Crossing times: Portsmouth-Ryde 25min. Lymington-Yarmouth 30min. Portsmouth-Fishbourne 45min
Frequency: Around the clock, with a summer peak of 130 crossings daily

ESTUARIAL SERVICES
Humber Ferry, Hull-New Holland
This service was withdrawn on 24 June 1981, when the new Humber road bridge was opened to traffic

Tilbury-Gravesend Ferry
Crossing time: 5min
Frequency: 20min (peak), 30min (off-peak)

LAKE SERVICE
Lake Windermere (Passenger Service)
Frequent service during Easter Holidays and from 2 May until 3 October (1982)
Journey times: Lakeside-Bowness 35min; Lakeside-Ambleside 75min; Bowness-Ambleside 30min; Round the Lake 2hr 40min

Note: Of the above list, the following services are in conjunction with French Railways (SNCF): Dover/Folkestone-Calais/Boulogne/Dunkerque; Newhaven-Dieppe* and the Dover-Dunkerque Train Ferry. The Dover/Folkestone-Ostend service is run in conjunction with Régie des Transport Maritimes (RTM). The Harwich-Hook of Holland service is run in conjunction with the Zeeland Steamship Co. One ship, the *Saint Eloi* on the Dover-Dunkerque service is owned by Sealink's subsidiary ALA.

* The Newhaven-Dieppe service was under review when this book went to press, pending a new agreement between the SNCF and Sealink UK Ltd.

4. A Review of Recent Operations

Continental Services

The years 1980/81 witnessed fierce competition on all the routes, despite the worsening economic recession in the UK. Following the curtailment of the pooling arrangement with TTF, there has been an intensive marketing campaign aimed at developing the passenger and accompanied car traffic on the Dover/Folkestone-Calais/Boulogne routes. The delivery delays of the two new ferries, *St Anselm* and *St Christopher* seriously affected 1980 traffic on the Dover-Calais service and to make matters worse Sealink's competitors were able to introduce new or additional tonnage in time for that summer's season; thus temporarily gaining a significant marketing advantage, particularly for accompanied car traffic. However 1981 saw both ships enter service, and these long-awaited new ferries have restored

Sealink's capacity to increase its share of the market, as was demonstrated by *St Anselm* in the first six months of her service, during which she made a considerable impact upon customers, especially the roll-on, roll-off service for freight.

In 1980 a considerable loss of traffic was caused by the blockade of ports in August by striking French fishermen (a disruption shared of course by the competitors) and there was much inconvenience to customers over this crucial holiday period. Luckily Sealink UK Ltd was better placed than some of its competitors and was able to divert traffic via Belgian ports. Many additional services were run at this time via Ostend in conjunction with the French and Belgian partners in Sealink; albeit at extra cost.

With the delivery of the 7,003ton

St Christopher to the Dover-Calais service, Sealink christened their ships on this route as the 'Flagship Service' for advertising purposes, in the early summer of 1981, as part of an intensive advertising campaign. A new SNCF ship, the *Cote d'Azur* was delivered to the route on 7 October 1981.

The tourist trade is notoriously affected by the state of national economies, and the high level of inflation in the UK in 1980/81, with the strong pound and high cost of hotel accommodation etc, coupled together to make Britain a less attractive place to visit for a holiday, in the eyes of the Continental tourist. Conversely the

96 Launching the 7,003ton *St Christopher* at the Belfast shipyard of Harland & Wolff. This multi-purpose ferry went into the Dover-Calais 'flagship' service in May 1981, to join the sister ship *St Anselm*.
Harland & Wolff

traffic from the UK to France expanded considerably, particularly the day excursion traffic. In 1981 prices in many south of England restaurants, for example, had risen to the extent that it actually worked out cheaper to take a day trip across the Channel, have lunch in a restaurant in Calais, Boulogne or Dieppe and return home in the evening!

The economic recession in the UK has of course hit the freight market and this factor, combined with the late delivery of the two new ships adversely affected the carrying on the short sea routes (Dover/ Folkestone-Calais/Boulogne/Dunkerque); however 1981 has seen an improvement, with the two ships in service. Traffic in new cars, chassis and caravans for export and import was also down because of the recession, in particular because of a drop in sales in the UK and on the Continent. In 1981 a vigorous campaign to draw attention to the attractions of the Weymouth-Cherbourg service was launched. This route is now operated by Sealink UK Ltd. A decision to withdrawn from the Newhaven-Dieppe service (leaving this to the SNCF to run alone) caused a staff dispute in the first weeks of 1982, with the *Senlac* used as a blockade at Newhaven for five weeks, pending a successful solution. This route suffered badly in 1981, losing over £1million.

Channel Islands Services
A generally healthy picture was created over the period by these services, with a growth of 15% in 1980, whereas the competitive airlines suffered a decline in the market share. This was due in part to an attractive variety of off-peak offers made in conjunction with the Channel

97

97 The 6,268ton *Galloway Princess*, introduced on the Stranraer-Larne service in May 1980. This was the first of four new ships ordered from Harland & Wolff's Belfast yard, at a total cost of £64million. The last to be delivered was the 7,000ton *St David,* which entered service on the Holyhead-Dun Laoghaire route in August 1981. *Harland & Wolff*

98 Isle of Wight services, with the *Shanklin* (now withdrawn) in the foreground and the car-ferry *Caedmon* beyond. The Portsmouth-Fishbourne route is to get two new 1,800ton large capacity car ferries in 1983, with room for up to 142 cars each, almost double the number carried by the largest of the present ferries. Passenger capacity will be 1,000. The passenger ship *Shanklin* was sold in 1980

to the Waverley Preservation Society, and renamed the *Prince Ivanhoe,* for use as a pleasure steamer. Sadly, she struck rocks in the Gower Peninsula, and sank, less than a year later with 400 holidaymakers rescued. One passenger died, of a heart attack, after rescue. *Ambrose Greenway*

99 The Heysham–Isle of Man service is worked by the 3,589ton motor vessel *Manx Viking,* built in 1976. Considerable improvement in patronage has been a feature of this route since 1980, when Sealink took over operations from Manx Line (Holdings) Ltd. *ISR*

100 Sealink's 'Freshwater' fleet, on the Lake Windermere services are a quartet of elegant and highly popular vessels, the

98

99

100

101

Tern, Swift, Teal and Swan. The year 1982 will commemorate 110 years of services on the lake, and in 1981, the Tern celebrated her 90th birthday. Despite her age the ship is in such an excellent condition, due to the pride and care of the staff, that this eldest member of the Sealink fleet may well live on to celebrate her 'century, not-out'! The Tern was built in 1891 for the Furness Railway, at Wivenhoe in Essex. Nowadays she has a diesel engine replacing the original steam boiler (which was built at Barrow). *Sealink UK Ltd*

101 When the new Humber road bridge was opened to traffic in June 1981, the Sealink vehicle and passenger ferry between Hull and New Holland was withdrawn. In final days the service was worked by the diesel-electric paddle vessel *Farringford* (seen here) originally built for the Isle of Wight service between Lymington and Yarmouth (in 1948) but for many years the Humber Ferry was the province of the attractive paddlesteamers (see photos 67, 68). *Ambrose Greenway*

Islands hoteliers and Tourist Officers. Car-carrying trade remained constant, and there was a growth in the carriage of commercial road vehicle traffic. In March 1981 the 4,478ton *Earl Granville* was introduced to the Portsmouth-Channel Islands service, and the *Earl William* was transferred to the Weymouth-Channel Islands route.

The Republic of Ireland Services
Despite a poor tourist season in 1980, and an increased competition in the shape of the B & I Company's new passenger and freight service from Pembroke to Rosslare, plus the Jetfoil service from Liverpool to Dublin, a good level of business has been retained. In the case of the Fishguard-Rosslare freight service carryings have increased, despite the recession in the UK. 1980 was a record year for passenger traffic, with 1.5 million passengers carried on the two routes to the Republic. The new 7,000 ton *St David* was introduced to the route from Holyhead-Dun Laoghaire in August 1981. Before this, Sealink chartered the Stena Line multi-purpose vessel *Princess Desiree*, of 5,793ton, to provide adequate capacity for the summer 1981 traffic

102 **Completely dwarfed by the huge and ugly Lykes Line barge carrier *Tillie Lykes*, the motorvessel *Catherine* of the Tilbury-Gravesend ferry service comes alongside at Gravesend.** *Ambrose Greenway*

because of the late delivery of the *St David* from Harland & Wolff.

Northern Ireland Services
In May 1980 the new 6,268ton ferry *Galloway Princess* was introduced to the Stranraer-Larne route, and this large multi-purpose ship has boosted carryings, in all categories, to record levels. Conversely, despite the charter of two higher capacity vessels to promote the Heysham-Belfast roll-on, roll-off service in early 1980, plus an intensive marketing campaign, Sealink UK Ltd concluded that there was no prospect of achieving profitability on this route and the service was withdrawn in December 1980 with losses for the year over the £1million mark.

Isle of Wight Services
As well as providing an all-the-year round service for the inhabitants of the island, for freight as well as passengers, these services are extremely popular with holidaymakers and the accompanied car and passenger traffic continues to grow. In order to assess the design for future ships, needed to replace the ageing existing vessels on the Portsmouth-Ryde route, a high speed catamaran was chartered for a short period in 1980, and this was the subject of generally favourable customer and staff reaction. Two new car ferries for the Portsmouth-Fishbourne service have been authorised for delivery in 1983 together with new

terminal facilities. On 7 June 1980, Sealink celebrated 150 years of the Lymington-Yarmouth service.

Isle of Man Service
During 1980, Sealink UK Ltd increased its shareholding in Manx Line from 60% to 85% and changed the management structure of the company which is now known for publicity purposes as Sealink Isle of Man. A substantial increase in traffic carrying was a feature of 1980, with passenger traffic up by over 60%, accompanied cars by over 50% and commercial vehicles by over 100% compared to the previous year. Of the total market to the Isle of Man, the Company then had 40% of the passenger market and 60% of the freight.

Other Services
On Lake Windermere, in June 1981, the *Tern*, oldest and smallest ship in the Sealink fleet, celebrated her 90th birthday. About 0.75million holiday makers are carried each year by the four ships on the lake.

The Secretary of State for Transport accepted the recommendation of the Transport Users' Consultive Committee that the Humber Ferry service between Hull and New Holland, operated by Sealink, should be closed after the opening of the Humber Bridge. This event took place on 24 June 1981, with the DEPV *Farringford* making a final public excursion that evening.

102

Pictorial Interlude : Portrait of a Flagship

Sealink UK Ltd has approximately 10,177 staff. Of these 56% are land-based and 44% are on board ship (1980 figures). It would require a complete book of its own to portray the multitude of activities required to run the day-to-day affairs of this great concern. In choosing to portray a 'Flagship' of the fleet, and some of the people involved in her operation, I am intending this as a 'salute' to all Sealink's staff, on land and sea.

103 **Officers and crew of the *St Christopher*, led by Capt Edwin Venables, pose on the passenger walkway.** *ISR*

103

60

Sealink

104

105

106

107

104 Senior Master of the *St Christopher*, Capt Edwin Venables, using the bridge wing controls to berth the ship at Calais. *ISR*

105 Second Officer Brian Buddle checks the course in the chartroom of the *St Christopher*. *ISR*

106 Radio Officer Bob Heard at his console on board *St Christopher*. *ISR*

107 Chief Engineer Bill Gibbons (right) discussing dial readings with Third Engineer Officer Eric Stankiste (left) in the engine control room of the *St Christopher*. *ISR*

108 Fourth Engineer Officer Dave Stroud checks the flow valves in the engine fuel purifying room on the *St Christopher*. *ISR*

109 *St Christopher* and sister ship *St Anselm* have a separate commercial vehicles driver's lounge and restaurant. Here, two Spanish drivers are being waited on by Assistant Steward Malcolm Baker. *ISR*

110

111

112

113

114

110 Assistant Barmen Tony Goldsmith (left) and Mervyn Elliot are kept busy at the bar of the *St Christopher*. *ISR*

111 Steward Ian Walker serves snacks and refreshments in the tea bar situated on the upper deck of *St Christopher*. *ISR*

112 *St Christopher's* cafeteria provides a selection of hot meals, snacks and drinks. Here, Assistant Stewards Derek Down (left) and Percy Bond keep things moving. *ISR*

113 The focal point for most cross-Channel passenger is the duty free shop. Here Barmen Graham Merricks (left) and Chris Dexter ensure quick service. *ISR*

114 Shop attendant Penny Pepino serving perfumes and other goods in the *St Christopher's* gift shop. *ISR*

115 Purser Bob Bewley (left) and Assistant Purser Roy Skelton handle passenger enquiries from the Information Office. *ISR*

116 AB's George Stupple (left) and Bill Dyer take in securing lines whilst casting off at Calais. *ISR*

115

116

5. Ports and Harbours

Ports and Harbours

This review is chiefly concerned with the ports and harbours owned by Sealink, but some of the other ports used by their services are included.

Sealink UK Ltd owns and operates seven of the major ports which serve the fleet. These are: Harwich (Parkeston Quay), Fishguard, Folkestone, Newhaven, Holyhead, Heysham and Stranraer, as well as a number of minor harbours. All these ports are rail-connected as well as handling traffic originating by road. In the case of Fishguard the subsidiary company operates the port. Sealink's harbour operations, used not only by their own services, but also by other operators, are financially very viable. Receipts from harbour dues and handling and other services have however to be set against the costs of dredging, policing, repairs and improvements to the quays and buildings. A trading surplus of £3million was achieved in 1978, the last year of the Shipping and International Services Division.

All these ports have enjoyed substantial investment in recent years, and can offer a wide range of facilities, including modern passenger terminals, specialised roll-on/roll-off berths, high capacity cranes for containers, general cargo quays and even, in some cases, bases for oil exploration and oil supply companies.

At Harwich a scheme exists for the establishment of further new port facilities at Bathside Bay, by reclaiming mud flats, owned by the British Railways Board, in conjunction with a Development Company. The existing port at Harwich Parkeston Quay has been completely modernised in recent years, with a new passenger terminal directly linked to the

118

117 Bridge-eye's view of the car-ferry ramp at Newhaven. Creation of roll-on, roll-off facilities has given new life and commerce to this port in particular; once threatened by closure when 'classic' passenger business declined, because of the growth of car-ownership. This picture makes a fascinating comparison with the view reproduced as photo 29. The railway still serves the port today, and the lines are in the righthand background, but it is the road vehicle which has mainly dictated the layout and modernisation of Newhaven.
Ambrose Greenway

118 Passengers disembarking at Parkeston Quay, Harwich in the early morning, from the *Avalon*; then (1965) the largest ship of the BR fleet, and used on the overnight Harwich-Hook of Holland service. This cold and often wet and windy transfer from ship to shore, or vice versa, for long one of the least attractive features of sea travel has undergone a transformation at the majority of the ports used by Sealink, in the last 10 years.
British Rail

railway station. Modernisation of passenger circulating areas, and their associated facilities and amenities, has been a feature of all Sealink's ports over the past decade, and also improved ramps and approach roads for vehicle loading. Good marshalling areas and covered accommodation for motorists, have featured largely in this general modernisation of the ports.

The ports used by, but not owned by, Sealink, in the UK and at the outer destinations of their services, have also been modernised by their respective owners or operators in recent years, and indeed it is true to say that this aspect of sea-travel and the sea-borne transit of freight has been revolutionised. No longer is the port a bleak and blustery wasteland, with a bewildering lack of information signs, and by night full of mysterious dim lights and sounds. Today the ports offer clear signposting and comfortable waiting areas, with all the various services — the motoring organisations, bureau-de-change, information, ticket offices, etc, grouped together. The walk from this area to the ship itself is nowadays mostly under cover, including the gangway on the quayside. The motorist, of course, quite literally drives on board and simply climbs the stairs inside the ship; once he has driven through the Customs and passport control area.

To conclude, here is a summary of some recent port improvement schemes, affecting Sealink UK Ltd's services to their customers. It is by no means exhaustive, but will serve to give the reader some idea of what is involved. In some cases work is still in progress.

---

*Denotes port owned by Sealink UK Ltd
‡Port owned by subsidiary company

Boulogne
New Customs and Passport controls installed. Plans to extend ferry port, and construction of new ramp for tourist cars to the flight deck above the Gare Maritime.

Calais
New passenger terminal building opened in April 1980 and third two-tier (No 3) ferry berth. Large new parking areas for cars and commercial vehicles, on reclaimed land (a 5-year, £16million programme of improvements).

Dover
New double-deck, double-width berths constructed at Eastern Dock Ferry Terminal.

Fishbourne
New vehicle ferry ramp; further improvement to the modern associated terminal facilities, and inner harbour dredging.

Fishguard‡
Modifications costing £200,000 to vehicle loading and unloading facilities, including installation of a new side-loading ramp. New double width roadway for lorries, via north entrance.

Folkestone*
Ten-year, £1.25million, scheme to improve terminal facilities completed in July 1980, with the final stage being the extension and improvement of the passenger hall and provision of a new waiting area for 'classic' passengers.

Guernsey
New covered gangway for passengers from ship to shore.

Harwich (Parkeston Quay)*

New double width ramp installed to serve Prins Ferries, DFDS and other shipping companies. New high level walkways for all three berths used by passenger ships, with covered access from ship to terminal.

Ostend

New walkway installed, with enclosed gallery and baggage conveyor system.

Portsmouth

New £2million car ferry terminal under construction at Gunwharf Road, by City Council.

119 Harwich; before modernisation of the terminal facilities at Parkeston Quay. The ships are the *England* (nearest), the *Avalon* (centre) and the *Amsterdam*. The railway station is on the lower left of the picture. *B. Coaley*

120 The Vision — an architect's drawing of the proposed modernisation of Harwich Parkeston Quay, for a new two-storey passenger terminal building linked to the existing railway station and the modernised quayside with roll-on, roll-off loading. Note the covered walkway for foot passengers and covered gangway to ship. *British Rail*

121 The accomplishment — Harwich Parkeston quay. *ISR*

Rosslare

£5million development as Ireland's 'Europort', with new pier and second berth for ferries. Extensive new parking areas and new passenger facilities and offices are a part of the scheme.

Stranraer*

New port complex costing £4million, with new pier and double-deck ramp. New

approach road, marshalling areas and covered walkway for passengers leading to a new amenity building.

Weymouth

New Ferry Terminal opened spring 1980, together with new car park and new accommodation for Customs and Tourist Information services.

121

123

122   *122*   The new car ferry terminal complex at Calais occupies the foreground of this picture. The next stage of development, costing some £30million, will change the familiar profile of Calais harbour known to generations of cross-Channel travellers. The existing Eastern jetty will be removed and re-sited increasing the width of the Harbour mouth from its present 130m to 230m which will permit two vessels to enter or leave the port at the same time. It will also permit the construction of additional car ferry berths as required.
Calais Chamber of Commerce

123   Calais' new car ferry terminal building, viewed from the entrance, with vehicle waiting area in the foreground. The quay is beyond the building. Opened in April 1980, an estimated five million passengers and one million vehicles had used it by May of 1981. The terminal, largest and best equipped of its kind on the European mainland, has a surface area of some

9,000sq m on three levels. It is nine times larger than the building it replaced and provides a high standard of passenger comfort including a 100-seat restaurant, a 300-seat snack bar, a bar, large well appointed public waiting areas and other facilities.

The opening of the terminal building was the culmination of a five year, £16million programme, which effectively increased the surface area of the car ferry terminal complex sevenfold and has provided the finest facilities for handling freight, accompanied vehicles and passengers on the European mainland. Former car ferry berths have been replaced by modern two tier structures to accommodate the new generation of jumbo sized car ferries. Private cars and freight vehicles are segregated. Twenty five acres of pre-customs and immigration parking have been provided with a further 15 acres of parking for vehicles awaiting embarkation.
Calais Chamber of Commerce

125

124 Roll-on, roll-off facilities at Dover, with the new two-tier loading ramps in the top righthand of the picture.
Ambrose Greenway

125 Sealink's flagship, the *St Anselm* berthed at one of Dover's two new two-tier vehicle ramps. *Sealink UK*

126

127

128

126 Road entrance to the RTM/Sealink car ferry terminal at Ostend, for the Dover and Folkestone services. *Richard Capper*

127 Folkestone passenger terminal; passengers embarking for a Boulogne service are seen leaving the waiting area and entering the customs and passport control hall. Beyond that a covered walkway leads to the ship. *British Rail*

128 The foyer of the new passenger terminal at Folkestone, with bureau de change, tickets and information offices and other passenger facilities all grouped together in a pleasing modern environment. *British Rail*

129 The 7,836 tons passenger and vehicle ferry *St Columba*, dressed overall for her inaugural sailing, positively dwarfs the quayside at Holyhead; May 1977. The new rail-sea passenger terminal facilities are seen in the left foreground (then nearing completion) with the trains beyond. *British Rail*

6. Sealink's Corporate Image

A strong feature of today's Sealink group is its immediately recognisable corporate image including the brand name of Sealink, which has become firmly established in the public's mind. This has largely come about by means of a deliberate and well planned design policy; first introduced in 1964 by the then Chairman of the British Railways Board, Dr Richard Beeching. Prior to this, the BRB had setup a Design Panel to advise on all matters concerning industrial and graphic design and this Panel had been able to appoint outside consultants to assist with the interior furnishing and layout of all new ships, commencing with the *Maid of Kent,* in 1959; as described later.

Dr Beeching came to the railways from ICI, a large and successful outside industry, and he brought with him a determination to rid BR of its last vestiges of steam-age imagery in the public's mind. When compared to the airlines, for example, the colours and symbols of the trains and ships (or rather, the *lack* of colour, in the case of the ships) were, he considered, both drab and unimaginative.

In a *Financial Times* article, appearing under his signature, at the end of April 1964, Dr Beeching gave the public the first news of a comprehensive new corporate identity then being prepared for British Railways by their Design Panel. In fact the BRB's then Director of Industrial Design, Mr George Williams, commissioned one of Britain's leading industrial design firms, Design Research Unit headed by Professor Misha Black, to undertake this very considerable task. In his article, Dr Beeching said that he personally considered that the essentials in the achievement of a new image for BR were a 'mark' powerful enough to

symbolise the service it stands for; a distinctive namestyle and logotype for the title of the undertaking, together with good legible subsidiary lettering styles, and a distinctive range of 'house colours' for use throughout the system.

Thus was born the present-day BR symbol of two-way traffic arrows; the namestyle 'British Rail' (and later, of course, Sealink) and the 'house colours' of rich monastral blue, mid-grey, white and flame red. New letterforms were devised for all signs and notices, and a general improvement in the quality of printed publicity was also established. A comprehensive 'House-style' manual was produced by the Design Panel to guide all concerned in the day-to-day application of the corporate identity elements.

Initially there was a degree of hostile public reaction to the new symbol and colours, perhaps predictably, but they

131

132

130 The 'two-way arrow' symbol of British Rail, in metal, painted white, upon the flame red funnel of the *Ailsa Princess*. In this particular case the parallel white bands are continued around the funnel to make a decorative feature. The top arrow normally points to the right (as seen here) but on the other side of the funnel it is reversed in order to point to the front of the ship. This is the only time the BR symbol points the opposite way. (See picture 157 of the *St Anselm* for an example.)
Ambrose Greenway

131 A powerful symbol — the 'two-way arrow' of BR and a bold namestyle (or logotype) — the Sealink image. These corporate identity elements are seen here on the *Caesarea*, berthed at Newhaven.
Ambrose Greenway

132 Each of the partners in the Sealink consortium retains its own symbol and house flag, allied to the use of the word Sealink painted on the hull sides. The RTM symbol, in light blue with dark blue outline is seen here on the pale yellow funnel, with black top. The ship is the *Prins Philippe*.
Ambrose Greenway

133 The sheer size of the lettering ensures legibility over considerable distances, and the word Sealink is recognisable even when partially obscured, as seen here the SNCF/Sealink car ferry *Villandry*. The ships of the Newhaven-Dieppe service are painted in the blue and white livery, but the funnel is yellow with a black top and carries the distinctive house flag of this Anglo-French service, dating back to the first railway companies who operated it.
Ambrose Greenway

133

soon gained widespread acceptance when it became obvious how much brighter and more cheerful the railway scene was becoming. In fact, it was the BR shipping fleet that demonstrated this transformation most rapidly and effectively. Because ships receive regular repainting in the constant combat against the effects of sea-environmental corrosion, it was possible to have some 20 ships of the BR fleet in the new colours in the first few months of this comprehensive scheme. The change, from black to rich blue for the hull, from buff yellow to flame red for the funnel — and with the new symbol in white on the red funnel and on the blue house flag — was indeed dramatic.

The first of the repainted ships had the main superstructure, above the blue hull, painted in a light blue-grey shade. Although a very attractive colour, the masters of the ships concerned soon voiced their concern that this blue-grey was making their ships less visible to others in bad weather or light conditions and so their views were heeded and the blue-grey was changed to white; incidentally making them even more attractive, in the present writer's opinion!

As already described, the decision to paint the brand-name Sealink on the ships' sides (in the standard sans-serif alphabet adopted by BR) was an important further step in establishing the shipping services of BR clearly in the public's eye. Before this, the BR 'arrow' symbol on the funnel and on publicity material of all kinds, had already made the impact that Dr Beeching had desired. No longer were the ships of the railway fleet visually anonymous — now their identity was there, clear and loud for all to see! Many shipping concerns have since copied the bold

135

134

identity style that BR produced —
imitation, it is said, is the sincerest form of
flattery.

With the creation, in Britain originally,
of Sealink as a brand name for a service
involving a multi-consortium, the other
partners have come into line by using it
for all publicity and by painting it upon
the sides of their vessels. Now that Sealink
UK Ltd exists as a separate company,
within the BR structure, the use of the
'arrow' (railway) symbol has been reduced
somewhat (except on ships' funnels and
flags) but the main elements of the
corporate identity remain as before.

It is a testimony to the foresight and
wisdom of all who originally conceived the
scheme that, some 18 years or so later, it
still has such a compelling attraction to
the eye, and that it has been so widely
imitated by others, including the Sealink
consortium.

136

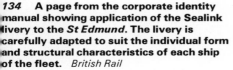

134 A page from the corporate identity
manual showing application of the Sealink
livery to the *St Edmund*. The livery is
carefully adapted to suit the individual form
and structural characteristics of each ship
of the fleet. *British Rail*

135 A page from the British Rail
Corporate Identity manual, showing the BR
logotype and Sealink brandname, as used
prior to the formation of Sealink UK Ltd;
nowadays the word Sealink is usually used
alone. *British Rail*

136 Logotype of the Harwich–Hook of
Holland Zeeland services. *Zeeland*

137 Logotype used by French Railways,
and painted in white upon the red of the
ships' funnels of the French-owned Sealink
ferries. *SNCF*

137

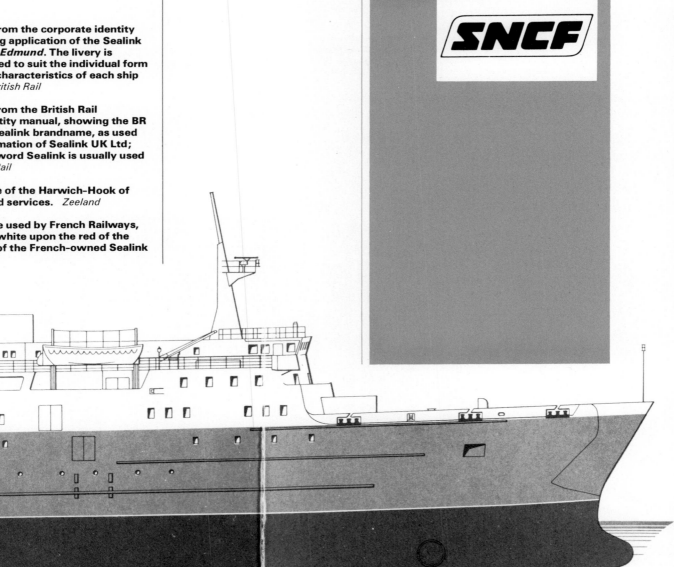

← Canterbury bar ♇

138

← Lounges

← Purser - Information ⓘ

← Ladies ♀

← Gentlemen ♂

139

↙ B Deck

Sealink shop
Restaurant ✕
Buffet ⬭
Bureau - de - change
Purser - Information ⓘ
Passport office
Lounge
Non smoking lounge
Ladies rest room
Cabins

↙ Car decks

**138/139 Examples of on-ship lettering
and the Sealink house-style.** *British Rail*

The Sealink Fleet

7. Three Decades of Design Development

Since the nationalisation of the British railway system and its associated shipping services, in 1948, the design of the ships for these services has undergone something of a revolution. This has been brought about by a fundamental social change of habit, and by technical progress in marine engineering and naval architecture.

This fundamental social change has, of course, been the widespread increase in car ownership. The car has become a major factor in many people's way of life; ranking second in importance only to the house, in terms of financial outlay and maintenance. People's attitude to travel and to holidays has changed accordingly. In 1948 it was a familiar sight at any main railway station or port, to see long queues of people laden with holiday luggage, waiting (perhaps patiently!) for a seat on a train, or a place on a boat. Throngs of

men, women and children struggled to find tickets, to read indicators, to queue at barriers with gates firmly closed, and finally to choke the corridors and gangways of desperately over-crowded holiday relief trains and extra-sailings. Nowadays the holiday queue is more likely to be a three-lane affair of crawling or stationary mechanised vehicles, polluting the environment on a by-pass, or at the entrance to an important holiday town or city — such is progress!

The ships of the railway fleet when nationalised, in January 1948, were in the main of prewar origin, and these had mostly been refitted for civilian use after return to their owners from Admiralty requisition during 1939-45. They were mostly twin-screw, turbine steamships, with the layout of 'miniature liners', and with the majority of passengers being the 'classic' ones (ie not accompanied by his or her car). Indeed the amenities offered by these ships warranted their description of scaled-down liners. Their passengers had (usually) a choice of first, second or third class accommodation, with lounges, smokerooms and bars. A restaurant service and a tea room or cafeteria was normally a feature, and for the longer night journeys, the ships used had a large number of cabins and berths. When it became possible to build new ships such as, for example, the *Cambria* and *Hibernia*, for the Holyhead-Dun

Laoghaire service in 1949, the passenger accommodation was still to this pattern (significantly, perhaps, the London Midland Region chose to power these ships with diesel engines). There were two-berth cabins de luxe with wc and bath; one- and two-berth cabins; four- and six-berth cabins, plus open berths for third class passengers.

On the short sea routes, however, the build-up in motorcar traffic was already sufficient for the SR to adapt a ship to meet this demand, soon after the war. Just before the war broke out the LMSR had inaugurated the Stranraer-Larne service using a new stern-loading car ferry, the *Princess Victoria* (the first of two ill-fated ships of her name), the first ferry designed as a stern-loading car ferry to operate from UK shores. Following this pattern on the SR the *Dinard* was chosen for conversion and a tremendous amount of work was involved. During the war the *Dinard* had been a hospital ship and later a troop ship; finally becoming a prisoner-of-war carrier. In June 1947 she emerged from the yard of Palmers of Hebburn-on-Tyne drastically rebuilt as a car ferry vessel, with room for 70-80 cars and 300 passengers. Two car decks were installed with a turntable on the main deck which allowed unloading to be carried out on the 'first-on, first-off' principle. Meanwhile however, the majority of new ships built continued to be for passengers and cargo,

140 The *Vortigern*, contre-jour.
Ambrose Greenway

141 Wartime losses made it necessary for the British railway companies, and their continental associates, to order quite a few new ships, to reinstate their services. Ordered by the GWR, but delivered after nationalisation, the 3,481 ton twin-screw steam turbine passenger and cargo ship *St Patrick* was built by Cammell-Laird at Birkenhead, for the Fishguard-Rosslare service. *British Rail*

142

but in 1951, on 14 December to be precise, the first *new* drive-on, drive-off car ferry to be built for the BTC was launched by William Denny & Bros Ltd at Dumbarton.

The *Lord Warden*, a steam turbine ship of 3,333 gross tons had accommodation for 120 cars and 700 one-class passengers, and was built specifically for the Dover-Boulogne service. (An interesting fact is that the stabilisers that should have been fitted during building were used instead on the new Royal Yacht *Britannia* and the *Lord Warden* ran her first year in service without stabilisers fitted.) The layout of the *Lord Warden* demonstrated a changing attitude on the part of the BTC and the Southern Region towards its passenger amenities, in particular by being a one-class only ship, with extensive lounge seating.

The 10 years from 1955-65 witnessed a number of new 'classic' ships being introduced for the longer sea routes. In particular, there were the three 'Dukes' on the Heysham-Belfast route (1956) and the *Avalon* for the Harwich-Hook of Holland service (1963). These were still powered by the oil-fired steam turbine, and so too were the two new sister ships for the Channel Islands service, *Caesarea* (1960) and *Sarnia* (1961). The SNCF fleet was by now tending to favour diesel engines, and these were a feature of their train ferry *Saint Germain* (1951) and the car ferry *Compiègne* (1958), although their *Côte d'Azur* (1951) and their *Lisieux* (1953) were passenger steamships, and destined

to be the last of their kind built for the French services.

The steam turbines gave smooth and vibration-free propulsion, and gave the ships a fine turn of speed, but they were fuel-thirsty and the more economical, but slower, diesel engine began to be an attractive proposition. It brought with it new problems of vibration and noise, but in due course it was to prove its worth, and Sealink bade farewell to its last steamship, the *Maid of Kent* in the autumn of 1981. As a comparison to today's diesel-powered fleet it is interesting to see in the table below how the BR ships and those of her neighbours were powered in 1965:

142 The *Cambria*, second of the two new ships built for the London Midland Region's Holyhead-Dun Laoghaire service; seen after launching at the Harland & Wolff shipyard in Belfast on 21 September 1948 and being taken-over by tugs. *Ian Allan Library*

143 The *Dinard*, photographed soon after conversion to a car ferry in 1947 by the Southern Railway, for use on the Dover-Boulogne service, (which she opened on 1 July 1947). She was subsequently sold in 1959 and renamed *Viking*, for service in the Baltic; lasting until 1974. This stern-loading car ferry foreshadowed the future trend for the cross-Channel routes at a time when the 'classic' passenger still predominated. *British Rail*

Titled trains on British Railways operated in connection with BR steamers (1953)

Southern Region	Night Ferry	London (Victoria)-Paris (Nord)
	Golden Arrow	London (Victoria)-Dover
	Continental Express	London (Victoria)-Dover
	Continental Express	London (Victoria)-Folkestone
	Continental Express	London (Victoria)-Newhaven
Western Region	Irish Mail (via Fishguard)	London (Paddington)-Fishguard
London Midland Region	Irish Mail	London (Euston)-Holyhead
	The Ulster Express	London (Euston)-Heysham
	The Northern Irishman	London (Euston)-Stranraer
Eastern Region	The Hook Continental	London (Liverpool St)-Parkeston Quay
	The Day Continental	London (Liverpool St)-Parkeston Quay
Scottish Region	The Irishman	Glasgow-Stranraer

Note: With the exception of the SR London (Victoria)-Newhaven boat train, sometimes worked by an electric locomotive, all the above trains were steam-hauled in 1953.

British Railways sea routes and the ships in use in January 1965
Lake steamers, tugs and dredgers are not included in this list

Key to Abbreviations
MV Motor vessel   P Passenger   VF Vehicle ferry   SS Steamship   C Cargo   PS Paddle steamer   TF Train ferry

Route and Ship	Type	Gross tonnage	Purpose	Speed (knots)	Year built	Remarks
HARWICH-HOOK OF HOLLAND						
Amsterdam	SS	5,092	P/C	22½	1950	
Arnhem	SS	5,008	P/C	22½	1947	
Avalon	SS	6,584	P/C	22½	1963*	*Fitted with stabilisers
Koningin Emma	MV	4,353	P/C	21	1939	
Koningin Wilhelmina	MV	6,228	P/C	23	1960*	} Owned by Zeeland
Prinses Beatrix	MV	4,353	P/C	21	1939	} Steamship Co
HARWICH-ANTWERP/ROTTERDAM						
Colchester	MV	866	C	15	1959	
Isle of Ely	MV	866	C	15	1958	
HARWICH-ZEEBRUGGE						
Cambridge Ferry	MV	3,294	TF/C	14¼	1963	Fitted with stabilisers
Essex Ferry	MV	3,242	TF/C	14	1957	
Norfolk Ferry	MV	3,157	TF/C	14¼	1951	
Suffolk Ferry	MV	3,134	TF/C	14½	1947	
DOVER-DUNKERQUE						
Hampton Ferry	SS	2,989	TF/C/P	16½	1934	
Saint Germain	MV	3,094	TF/C/P	18½	1951	Owned by French Railways
Shepperton Ferry	SS	2,996	TF/C/P	16½	1935	
Twickenham Ferry	SS	2,839	TF/C/P	16½	1934	Owned by British/French subsidiary company
DOVER/FOLKESTONE-CALAIS/BOULOGNE						
Compiègne	MV	3,467	VF	21	1958	} Owned by French Railways
Côte d'Azur	SS	3,999	P	25	1951	}
Invicta	SS	4,191	P	22	1940	Fitted with stabilisers
Lord Warden	SS	3,333	VF	20	1952	Fitted with stabilisers
Maid of Kent	SS	3,920	VF	20¾	1959	Fitted with stabilisers
Maid of Orleans	SS	3,777	P	22	1949	Fitted with stabilisers
Normannia	SS	2,219	VF	19½	1952	Fitted with stabilisers

143

Route and ship	Type	Gross tonnage	Purpose	Speed (knots)	Year built	Remarks
NEWHAVEN-DIEPPE						
Arromanches	SS	2,404	P	25	1946	Flies French flag
Brighton	SS	2,875	P	24	1950	
Falaise	SS	2,416	P/VF	20½	1947	Fitted with stabilisers
Lisieux	SS	2,943	P	25	1953	Flies French flag
Nantes	MV	1,053	C	15	1946	Flies French flag
Rennes	MV	1,053	C	15	1947	Flies French flag
WEYMOUTH/SOUTHAMPTON-CHANNEL ISLANDS						
Caesarea	SS	4,174	P/C	20	1960	Fitted with stabilisers
St Patrick	SS	3,460	P/C	20	1948	
Sarnia	SS	4,174	P/C	20	1961	Fitted with stabilisers
Elk	MV	795	C	14	1959	
Moose	MV	795	C	14	1959	
Roebuck	SS	866	C	12¼	1925	
Winchester	MV	1,149	C	15	1947	
FISHGUARD-WATERFORD						
Great Western	SS	1,509	C	14	1934	
FISHGUARD-ROSSLARE						
St Andrew	SS	3,035	P/C	21	1932	
St David	SS	3,783	P/C/VF	20¾	1947	
HOLYHEAD-DUN LAOGHAIRE						
Cambria	MV	4,972	P/C	21	1949	Fitted with stabilisers
Hibernia	MV	4,972	P/C	21	1949	Fitted with stabilisers
Princess Maud	SS	2,917	P/C	20	1934	Replaced in 1965
HEYSHAM-BELFAST						
Duke of Argyll	SS	4,797	P/C	21	1956	Fitted with stabilisers
Duke of Lancaster	SS	4,797	P/C	21	1956	Fitted with stabilisers
Duke of Rothesay	SS	4,780	P/C	21	1956	Fitted with stabilisers
HEYSHAM-BELFAST AND HOLYHEAD-DUBLIN						
Container Enterprise	MV	982	C	12½	1958	⎫ Designed to carry 65
Container Venturer	MV	982	C	12½	1958	⎭ large-type containers
Slieve Bawn	SS	1,573	C	17	1937	
Slieve Bearnagh	SS	1,485	C	17	1936	
Slieve Bloom	SS	1,297	C	16	1930	
Slieve Donard	MV	1,598	C	16	1959	
Slieve League	SS	1,369	C	17	1935	
Slieve More	SS	1,370	C	16	1932	
STRANRAER-LARNE						
Caledonian Princess	SS	3,630	P/C/VF	20½	1961	Fitted with stabilisers

The larger ships of the estuarial services

FIRTH OF CLYDE

Glen Sannox	MV	1,107
Queen Mary II	SS	1,014
Duchess of Hamilton	SS	801
Duchess of Montrose	SS	794
Waverley	PS	693
Caledonia	PS	623

HAMPSHIRE-ISLE OF WIGHT

Brading	MV	837
Southsea	MV	837
Shanklin	MV	833
Sandown	PS	684

But now we must briefly retrace our steps to the commencement of the decade under review, because the influence of the motorcar was causing a need to rethink the services offered on some routes. A particular example was the Newhaven-Dieppe service, where the decline in 'classic' passenger trade was so dramatic that the service was under threat of complete closure, and with it the railway-owned port of Newhaven; a threat which hung in the balance for some years. On the short-sea crossings, the new SNCF car ferry *Compiègne* and the BTC's car ferry *Maid of Kent* (introduced in 1958/9 respectively) joined the *Lord Warden*, and quickly demonstrated their worth; with a steady growth in the business of car and coach carrying. The BTC realised that other routes would benefit if the drive-on, drive-off facility for cars and coaches could be adopted; but there were limits to the capital available for new ships and port installations. A solution was found in the conversion of existing 'classic' passenger ships of recent build, to become stern-loading or side-loading car ferries, as well as ordering some new purpose-built vessels, such as the *Dover* (1965) and *Holyhead Ferry I* (1965).

144

144 The *Lord Warden*, the first purpose-built car ferry ordered by the BTC, and delivered to the Dover-Boulogne route in June 1952. (The 'fireman's helmet' to her funnel was an addition made in 1957.) She is seen here in her final Sealink livery before withdrawal, with the *Holyhead Ferry I* in the background. The *Lord Warden's* days are not over yet, and she is now carrying pilgrims to Mecca! *Ambrose Greenway*

145 A selection of BTC ships, portrayed by the artist Charles King, on a poster published in 1957. Centre [2] is the handsome new *Duke of Rothesay*, perpetuating the 'classic' passenger ship tradition of the railway shipping services; but also portrayed [3] is the car ferry *Lord Warden* and [4] the train ferry *Norfolk Ferry*; emphasising the versatility of the BTC's shipping services, and incidentally making a fascinating contrast with some of the smaller vessels portrayed in the background! Of particular interest is [9] the *Bardic Ferry*, operated by the then BTC controlled Atlantic Steam Navigation Company (now Transport Ferry Service), a new custom-built stern-loading vehicle ferry, operating from Preston to Larne. This company had previously built-up a vehicle-carrying business using ex-tank landing ships. The *Bardic Ferry* and the similar *Ionic Ferry* also carried crane-loaded containers on their upper decks. *British Rail*

145

BRITISH TRANSPORT SHIPS

M.V. CAMBRIA	5 S.S. INVICTA	9 M.V. BARDIC FERRY	14 M.V. SHANKLIN	18 M.V. BROADFORD
S.S. DUKE OF ROTHESAY	6 M.V. GLEN SANNOX	10 M.V. BYLAND ABBEY	15 M.V. WINCHESTER	19 P.S. LINCOLN CASTLE
S.S. LORD WARDEN	7 S.S. BRIGHTON	11 M.V. WHITBY ABBEY	16 S.S. SLIEVE BAWN	20 M.V. SWAN
M.V. NORFOLK FERRY	8 S.S. NORMANNIA	12 S.S. ST. DAVID	17 P.S. MAID OF THE LOCH	21 D.E.P.V. FARRINGFORD
		13 S.S. AMSTERDAM		

146 The French Railway's steamship, the *Lisieux*, dressed overall for her maiden voyage from Dieppe, and seen entering Newhaven Harbour on 24 March 1953. When she entered service the days of the elegant 'classic' passenger cross-Channel vessels were already numbered, and her career with SNCF was not a long one; being withdrawn in June 1965 and sold. (See page 114 for details of her later career.)
British Rail

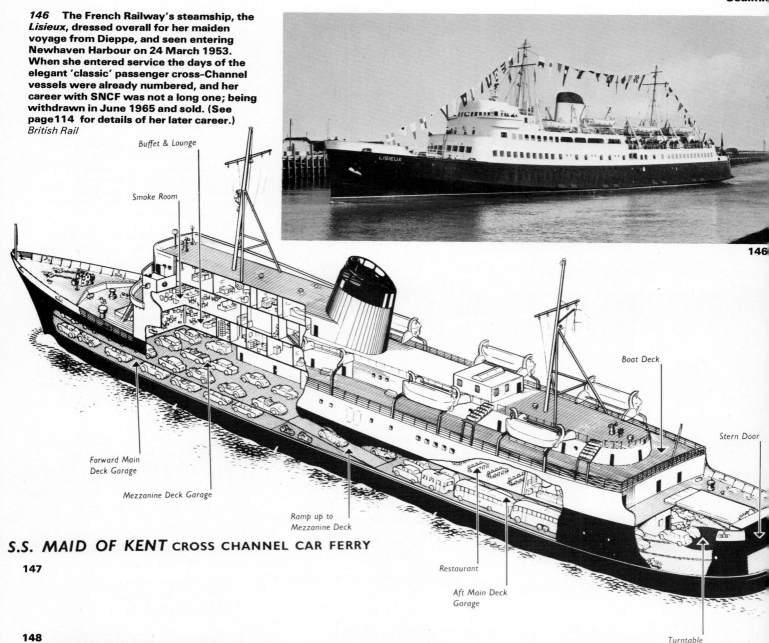

146

Buffet & Lounge

Smoke Room

Boat Deck

Stern Door

Forward Main
Deck Garage

Mezzanine Deck Garage

Ramp up to
Mezzanine Deck

Restaurant

Aft Main Deck
Garage

Turntable

S.S. *MAID OF KENT* CROSS CHANNEL CAR FERRY

147

148

It was the conversion in 1964 of the *Falaise*, which had been a passenger ship mainly intended for night service (with 1,527 passengers in two classes, including 338 sleeping berths), that rescued the Newhaven-Dieppe service from closure. In her new form she could carry 100 cars and 700 one-class passengers. Also converted on Tyneside at this time was the *Normannia*, for use on the Dover-Boulogne service. It gave these turbine steamships a further useful lease of life whereas unaltered they would have soon become redundant, faced with the steady decline in 'classic' passenger traffic and the closure of the Southampton-St Malo route. The *Falaise* boosted traffic on the Dieppe run until two new SNCF purpose-built car ferries, the *Villandry* and the *Valencay* were introduced in the summer of 1965.

What was by the mid-1960s also becoming an important factor in day-to-day commerce and transport was the development of the heavy-duty lorry and trailer (the 'juggernaut'), and the versatile freight container. The existing car ferries could usually carry a few coaches or other large vehicles near the stern, but their internal dimensions were most suited to the car and caravan. Trailer and lorry carrying was first developed on the Preston and Larne route (and later the Tilbury-Rotterdam routes) of the (then) BTC-controlled Atlantic Steam Navigation Company. This company had commenced operations soon after the end of the war with ex-tank landing ships, and in April 1954 had been taken over by the

147 The turbine steamship *Maid of Kent* was a purpose-built car ferry completed by William Denny & Bros Ltd at Dumbarton in 1959 for the Dover-Boulogne service. This stern-loading vessel (known when new as the 'Pocket Liner') could carry 190 cars and 1,000 one-class passengers. Her interior design and the layout of the passenger accommodation was the subject of special BTC attentions (see following chapter) and the *Maid of Kent* may be described as the first of the 'new wave' of BR car ferries in her design for the passenger. *British Rail*

148 The converted car ferry *Falaise* in full latterday Sealink livery, showing her large stern door. She was placed in service on the new Newhaven-Dieppe operation in 1964. The *Falaise* had been built as a passenger ship for the overnight Southampton-St Malo service, and her conversion to a car ·ferry gave new life to both the vessel, and the Newhaven-Dieppe service. *Ambrose Greenway*

149 The *Dover* and the basically similar *Holyhead Ferry I* went into BR service in 1965. These were stern-loading car ferries, following the pattern established by the *Maid of Kent*. The same year saw the SNCF introducing the car ferry *Villandry* for the Newhaven-Dieppe service. The era of the 'classic' ship was coming to a close. *British Rail*

150

BTC who soon provided it with two new purpose-built vehicle ferries, with stern loading; the *Bardic Ferry* and the *Ionic Ferry*. The undoubted success of this vehicle-carrying service was not lost upon the BTC's planners; it was becoming clear that there was considerable potential for a 'multi-purpose' ferry design, capable of carrying passengers, cars, trailers and lorries (and perhaps even railway wagons). The first stage of this

development was to produce ships with high trailer and lorry space; but still only stern loading.

At about this time it was also becoming desirable to give more room for car-carrying on the existing ships of the longer sea routes, and major conversion work was carried out upon a number of these, including the three 'Dukes' and the *Avalon*. The Channel Islands ships, *Sarnia* and *Caesarea*, were not so

altered however and lived-out their Sealink days as 'classic' ships.

It was the introduction of the bow visor, enabling loading through the bow, which made the Sealink ferries even more acceptable to the road haulier. The bow visor was developed in the early 1960s by Baltic ferry operators, and to begin with there was a degree of doubt as to its seaworthiness in English Channel or Irish Sea conditions. However, the arrival of the 'Viking' class ships on the Southampton-Cherbourg route demonstrated convincingly the advantage and practicability of the bow visor arrangement. The first BR ship to be built with a bow visor was the 1967 *Antrim Princess* for the Stranraer-Larne service. The bow and stern loading facility then became the norm for new ships in the late 1960s, and some existing ferries were rebuilt with bow visors to increase their versatility still further.

The concept of the 'multi-purpose' ferry, incorporating hoistable car decks in the high drive-through garage space, incidentally increasing capacity for cars, proved to be ideal for most of BR's shipping services, and one ship — the

T.S.S. "DUKE OF ROTHESAY"

CONVERSION TO PASSENGER/CAR FERRY, 1967, BY CAMMELL LAIRD (SHIPREPAIRERS) LIMITED. FOR BRITISH RAIL.

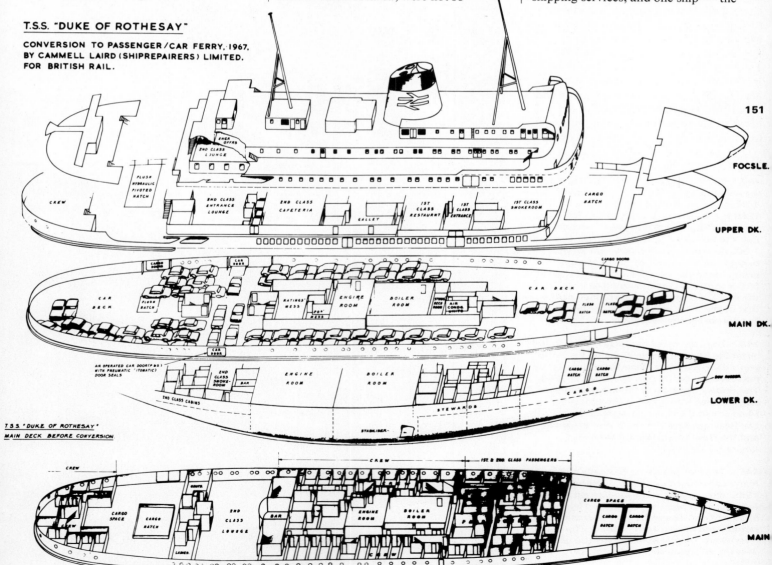

151

Vortigern (delivered in 1969) — took the 'multi-purpose' concept one stage further by having railway tracks on the main deck. This allowed the ship to switch routes. In winter it carried railway freight wagons between Dover and Dunkerque, and in summer it carried passengers and road vehicles between Dover and Boulogne.

The 'hot' and 'cold' political winds blowing around the Channel Tunnel project around the year 1969 had some restraining influence on new ship orders and design progress and by this time the BR Shipping and International Services Division were working on contingency plans for what would be required once (as then seemed very likely) the Tunnel would be built. Also at this time the Seaspeed hovercraft services were being enthusiastically developed and were creaming-off the 'classic' passenger trade. BR foresaw that as a result of a Channel Tunnel being built, taking the passenger trade, a fleet of multi-purpose ferries would be their best asset for the future. Meanwhile demand for vehicle carrying continued to grow year-by-year.

By the end of the 1970s (with the Channel Tunnel first of all definitely 'off' and then provisionally 'on' again!) the capacity requirements for roll-on, roll-off ferries had grown to such an extent that the designs of ferries had to allow room for lorries or trailers on *two* levels; each level having bow and stern access. These large capacity ships have been developed by clever use of the available space *within* the vessel, because the existing harbour facilities and sea depth (limiting draught) have prevented any dramatic further increase in the overall size of ships; as regards their length and breadth. Increased height has been more practicable, for the main superstructure, with the passenger accommodation placed on top of the two level vehicle space.

The four new Sealink vessels for the short sea services clearly demonstrate the

152

153

150   The elegant *Duke of Rothesay*, converted to a side-loading car ferry by Cammell Laird in 1967, (see next illustration).   *Ambrose Greenway*

151   Schematic view of the conversion of the *Duke of Rothesay* to a car ferry. *British Rail*

152   The 4,371ton MV *Vortigern*, built in 1969 for multi-purpose use as a car and passenger ferry, vehicle ferry and train ferry, according to the season of the year. *Ambrose Greenway*

153   The 5,590ton *Horsa* and her sister ship the *Hengist* were delivered in 1972 for the short sea routes, and were similar to the *Vortigern* except that no railway tracks were provided. Bow visors were fitted allowing a rapid roll-on, roll-off procedure for road vehicles.   *Ambrose Greenway*

remarkable progress in vehicle capacity that has been made in the last decade. The *St Anselm* for example, Sealink's new 'Flagship', and the similar *St Christopher*, are just about as large as can be accommodated in Dover Harbour but because of their two-level loading they can quickly turn around in that port some four or five times the vehicle capacity of their predecessors.

To conclude this brief survey of the past three decades, a complete description of the *St Anselm*, delivered to Sealink UK Ltd in November 1980, from Messrs Harland & Wolff of Belfast is given below. The *St Anselm* was named at their yard in Belfast on 4 December 1979 by Lady Parker, wife of the chairman of the BRB, and as the 'Flagship' of the fleet I have chosen this ferry to represent the best of Sealink UK Ltd's present day ships.

A Description of the 7,003ton MV St Anselm

MV *St Anselm* is a diesel engined twin screw passenger/vehicle ferry for Sealink UK Limited with the following principal dimensions:

Length overall: 129.4m
Length waterline: 125.5m
Length bp: 120.7m
Breadth moulded: 21.0m
Extreme over beltings: 21.6m
Depth to B deck: 13.2m
Deadweight: 1,755tonnes
Draught scantling: 4.72m
Service speed: 19.5kts

The ship is intended to operate between Dover and Calais, and the length overall, breadth extreme and draught are limited by terminal port restrictions.

The vessel is built under the survey of Lloyd's Register of Shipping requirements for a special Class + 100 A1 for Channel services and has a British Class II Certificate for 1,000 passengers and 72 crew for Short International Voyages.

The ship complies with the requirements of the British Department of Trade construction rules for passenger ships and also the 1960 SOLAS requirements including the amendments to the convention for fire protection and firefighting.

The Hull
St Anselm is of the roll-on, roll-off drive through type with two vehicle decks, bow visor and inner bow doors, stern door, twin bow thrusters, bow rudder, twin stern rudders, fin stabilisers, twin funnels and two self-supporting masts.

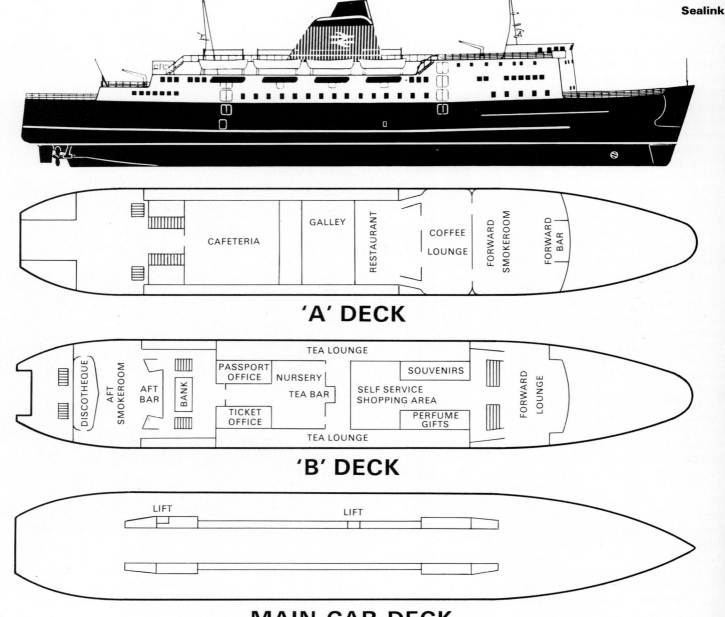

'A' DECK

CAFETERIA	GALLEY	RESTAURANT	COFFEE LOUNGE	FORWARD SMOKEROOM	FORWARD BAR

'B' DECK

TEA LOUNGE

DISCOTHEQUE · AFT SMOKEROOM · AFT BAR · BANK · PASSPORT OFFICE · NURSERY · TEA BAR · TICKET OFFICE · SELF SERVICE SHOPPING AREA · SOUVENIRS · PERFUME GIFTS · FORWARD LOUNGE

TEA LOUNGE

MAIN CAR DECK

LIFT   LIFT

154
155

A tea bar and lounge are situated on the promenade deck and on the boat deck there are forward, midship and aft lounges. A bar is provided in the forward lounge and a shop and duty free shop in the aft lounge. Further amenities include a passport office and a bank. Drivers of commercial vehicles have their own

154 Layout of the ferry *Hengist*, introduced 1972. *Sealink UK*

155 The car ferry *Holyhead Ferry 1*, renamed the *Earl Leofric* after conversion with bow visor. Photographed at Calais in September 1980. The *Dover* was similarly converted and renamed the *Earl Siward*. Both ships have now been replaced by the new multi-purpose ferries, and *Earl Leofric* was sold for scrap in 1981. *Richard Capper*

156 Cars and lorries being loaded on the *St George*, Harwich-Hook of Holland service. *British Rail*

157 Aerial view of *St Anselm*. *British Rail*

separate lounge and bar. All these spaces including passenger entrances and stairways from C deck to promenade deck have been designed and tastefully decorated by the decor consultants Ward Associates (see next chapter).

Two-berth cabins for 30 passengers are arranged on A and B decks.

The captain and chief engineer's suites, consisting of day cabin, toilet and lobby, are arranged on the promenade deck and have been designed by the decor consultants. Officers, petty officers and ratings' cabins have been arranged on the promenade deck, A deck, B deck and C deck to owners' requirements. A combined total of 62 commercial vehicles and 40 motor cars or 309 motor cars can be carried on the lower vehicle deck D and on the upper vehicle deck B.

Air conditioning is arranged to all passenger and crew accommodation and service spaces.

Six fibre-glass diesel-driven lifeboats are fitted and 20 inflatable liferafts are also provided.

The four new Harland & Wolff ships are the first Sealink ships with hydraulic deck machinery. Four automatically-driven tensioning winches are fitted, two forward and two aft, together with two windlass capstans fitted forward and two warping capstans fitted aft.

An automatic quartzoid bulb sprinkler and fire alarm system is fitted throughout the accommodation and service spaces. The system is sub-divided into sections, each fitted with its own set of controlling valves and all connected to an indicator in the Wheelhouse.

The lower and upper vehicle spaces are protected by a manually-operated

156

drencher system. The system is divided into sections, each controlled by a manually-operated valve.

Machinery
The vessel is propelled by two Crossley Pielstick 16-cylinder PC2V Mark 5 unidirectional marine propulsion engines and arranged to drive inboard turning controllable pitch propellers of Stone Manganese manufacture through flexible couplings and David Brown reduction gear units. Each engine produces a maximum continuous power output of 10,400bhp (metric) at 520rpm when burning any grade of fuel up to and

including 1,000 Secs Redwood No 1 at 38°C.

The gearboxes are built as handed pairs, horizontally offset with engines outboard and propellers inboard with input rpm of 520 and output rpm of 265. An integral thrust bearing of 100 tonnes capacity is fitted.

The crankcase is of a composite structure, fabricated by welding together cast steel and forged steel plates with intermediate plate sections. The gear case is of fabricated mild steel construction. Special attention is given to the stiffness of the double bottom and engine seatings.

A centralised cooling water system is

157

158   The Sealink 'Flagship', the 7,003ton *St Anselm*, with technical details:

Route: Dover-Calais
Builders: Harland & Wolff, Belfast
Yard Number: 1715
Length: 129.4m (oa), 125.5m (wi), 120.7m (bp)
Breadth: 21.6m (oa), 21m (mid)
Depth: 11.8m (upper deck)
Load draught: 4.65m
Scantling draught: 4.72m
Deadweight: 1,920tonnes
GRT: 7,003tonnes
NRT: 3,170tonnes
Service speed: 19.5kts
Passengers: 1,000
Crew: 72
Vehicle capacity: 28 × 12m RHVs or 122 cars (main garage, B deck); 34×12m RHVs and 40 cars *or* 187 cars (upper garage, D deck)
Clear deck heights: 4.42m (main and upper)

Passenger seats: 214 (lounge bar), 155 (aft bar), 286 (lounge griddle), 98 (tea/coffee lounges), 48 (driver's lounge), 156 (shelter deck), 76 (exposed deck)
Passenger berths: 18 (A deck), 12 (B deck)
Main Machinery: Two 16-cylinder Crossley Pielstick engines

Two Mk 5 medium speed diesels driving controllable pitch propellers via reduction gearboxes

   The ship is fitted with twin stern rudders, bow rudder, twin bow thrust units and stabilisers.

Key
1 Two Crossley-Pielstick medium-speed main engines
2 Transmission coupling and gearbox
3 Shaft alternators (port and starboard shafts)
4 Propeller pitch controls
5 C. P. propeller
6 Fin stabilisers (port and starboard)
7 Service pumps
8 Three Harland-M.A.N. diesel-driven alternators
9 Electrically-powered bow thrusters
10 Bow rudder and lock pin
11 Stern rudders (port and starboard)
12 Control room (engines and services)

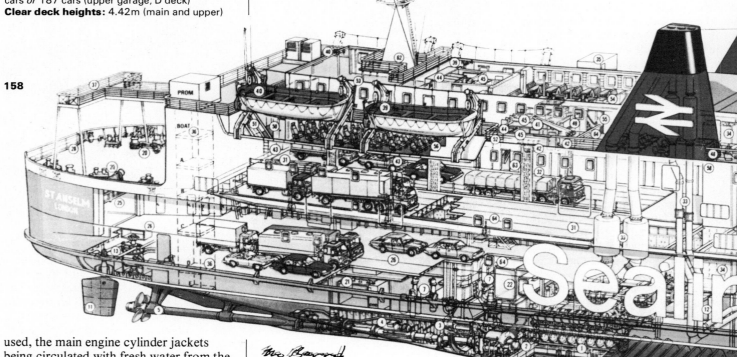

158

used, the main engine cylinder jackets being circulated with fresh water from the high temperature section and the air intercoolers, lubricating oil and fuel valve coolers with fresh water from the low temperature section.

   The 'dry sump type' lubrication system of each main engine is independent, as is the 'wet sump type' lubrication system of each gearbox.

   Each engine is provided with two water cooled exhaust gas turbo-chargers to which are fitted air intake filter silencers.

   Two reservoirs, charged by electric motor-driven compressors, supply air for starting main engines and diesel alternators.

   Two horizontal cylindrical oil fired multiple-pass water heaters provide hot water for ventilation and accommodation heating, the crew and passengers' hot water calorifier, indirect cylinders, engine warming heat exchangers, fuel tank heating and fuel rail tracing coils.

   Control of machinery is carried out from a control room and from the bridge.

   The auxiliaries are, in general, electric driven by single speed totally enclosed fan cooled motors.

The machinery installation is arranged in three watertight compartments with the diesel alternator and hot water heater compartment forward, the auxiliary machinery room situated under the control room, and the main engine room aft.

   The machinery is built and installed to comply in all respects with the latest Department of Trade regulations for the issue of a Class II Passenger and Safety Certificate, also to the requirements of

159   This view of the stern of the *St Anselm* taken at Calais shows clearly the two level vehicle deck arrangement, allowing simultaneous roll-on, roll-off activities for both. The funnels are set apart to the sides of the ship to give a clear internal layout, and a service lift is in the square housing on the righthand rear of the main superstructure. A comparison of the *St Anselm* of 1981 and ships of preceding stages of development and vehicle carrying capacity is given in accompanying tables.
Ambrose Greenway

13 Steering gear
14 Docking fender
15 Bow visor
16 Bow visor (raised, docked condition)
17 Bow visor hydraulic rams
18 Bow visor locks
19 Anchor handling machinery (port and starboard)
20 Mooring equipment and machinery
21 Sewage treatment plants
22 Lubricating oil tanks
23 Fuel oil tanks
24 Fresh water tanks
25 Stern vehicle loading door (main vehicle deck)

26 Main vehicle deck (D deck)
27 Bow vehicle loading doors
28 Bulwark gates (upper vehicle deck)
29 Forward garage door (upper vehicle deck)
30 Upper vehicle deck (B deck)
31 Four vehicle loading ramps (main to upper vehicle decks)
32 Hydraulic ram and chain-actuated ramps
33 Main and auxiliary engine exhaust outlets
34 Main services casing (control room to emergency alternator and damage control on promenade deck)
35 Service lifts (promenade to D deck)
36 Service lift (boat to main vehicle deck)
37 Foot passenger access at terminals

38 Lifeboats Nos 1 and 2
39 Accident lifeboats Nos 3 and 4
40 Lifeboats Nos 5 and 6
41 Liferaft stowage (port and starboard)
42 Liferaft davits and embarkation points (port and starboard 20 rafts, total capacity 500 persons)
43 Embarkation ladders (port and starboard)
44 Lifejacket lockers (port and starboard)
45 Toilets (port, centre and starboard)
46 Nursing mothers
47 Bank
48 Passport Office
49 Bureau
50 Gift shop
51 Duty-free shop and kiosk behind
52 First aid room
53 Promenade deck seated shelter
54 Tea lounge and tea bar
55 Boat deck, driver's lounge, bar and toilets (port)
56 Aft lounge
57 Midships lounges and servery
58 Lifejackets (starboard only)
59 Forward lounge, bar and gaming room
60 Captain, officers' quarters and radio room
61 Wheelhouse, also port and starboard wing control stands
62 Radar and radio communications masts
63 Main passenger staircases
64 Crew's quarters and ship's stores and workshops

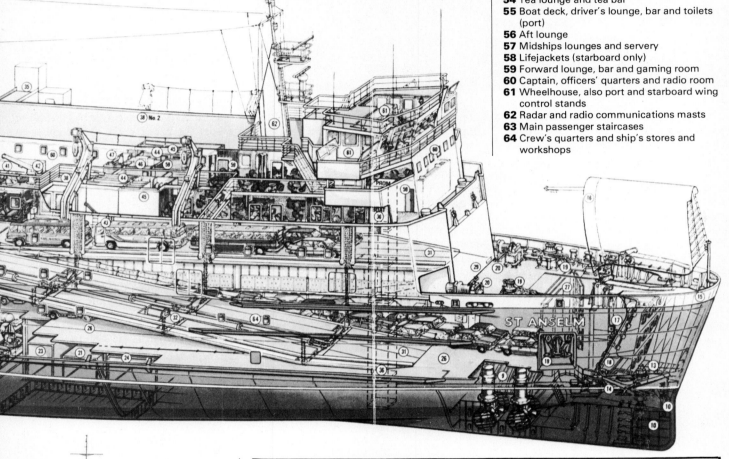

159

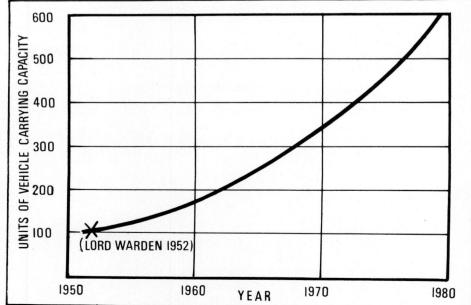

160

Lloyd's Register of Shipping and the Resolutions adopted by the Assembly of the Inter-Government Maritime Consultative Organisation in 1967.

Electrical Details
The power supplies for the electrical installation are provided by two main engine shaft-driven alternators rated at 1,200kW each, and three diesel-driven alternators rated at 675kW each, all at 415V, three-phase, 50Hz. In the event of power failure an automatic starting diesel-driven alternator rated at 330kW, 415V, three-phase, 50Hz is installed. The power distribution is arranged so that electricity for the normal sea load is provided by one of the shaft-driven alternators. On entering port this alternator is switched to supply the bow thrust unit, and the service load is supplied by the diesel-driven alternators.

The main switchboard controlling the five alternators is of the dead front self supporting deck mounted type manufactured by Harland and Wolff Ltd. Two group starter switchboards are also located in the machinery control room.

The engine room control console, together with the bridge executive and navigating consoles, are designed and manufactured by Harland and Wolff.

A bank of transformers 415/230V is fitted to provide supplies for lighting and heating in addition to hotel and small galley equipment.

Special attention has been paid to the requirements for illuminating the car decks and public rooms.

Equipment installed in addition to the main radio station and radars includes automatic pilot and gyro compass, echo sounder, speed and distance log, Decca navigator, rudder angle and windspeed and direction indicators together with communal aerial, fireproof and watertight door systems. Automatic and sound powered telephone installations and an extensive sound reproduction system are provided.

The most striking outward feature of these latest Sealink ferries is of course the placing of the two funnels one on either side of the ship's superstructure, giving a clear internal layout. A service lift to all decks is also a prominent feature.

The new SNCF ship for the Dover-Calais service, the 8,800 ton *Côte d'Azur* was launched at Le Havre by Ateliers et Chantiers du Havre on 22 December 1980 and was placed in service on 7 October 1981. This fine new ship completes the new look for the busy Dover-Calais service and gives Sealink a keen competitive fleet of modern ferries.

As this book was being written, the long-awaited Channel Tunnel was once again in favour, and an announcement that work was to commence was expected. No doubt, sooner or later, a tunnel *will* be built, but I am sure that these latest fine ships of the Sealink fleet have a long and busy career ahead of them — and it will be interesting to see what design developments take place over the next decade!

161

160   A general view of the interior of one of the two car decks on the *St Anselm*. Access to the passenger accommodation, and the trunking for machinery etc, is located on each side of the car decks. Hydraulic ramps give access between the upper and lower car decks, for use at ports not equipped with two-level loading and unloading facilities.   *Sealink UK*

161   The new SNCF ferry *Côte d'Azur*, which entered service on the Dover-Calais route in October 1981.   *SNCF*

162   The *St David*, last of the four new Sealink ferries to be completed at Harland & Wolff, and placed in service on the Holyhead-Dun Laoghaire route on 10 August 1981. A 7,000ton vessel, she can carry up to 1,000 passengers and 309 cars or 62×12m road haulage vehicles, or a mixture of the two, on two deck levels.   *ISR*

163   Plan and elevation of the SNCF/Sealink ferry *Côte d'Azur*, for the Dover-Calais service.   *SNCF*

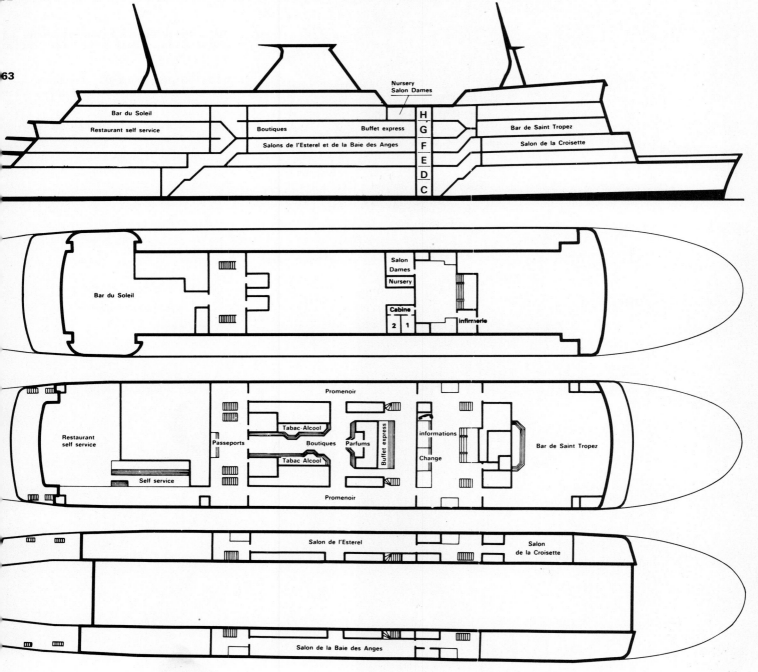

Pictorial Interlude : The Shipyard

The construction and launching of a new ship has a fascination all of its own. The great baulks of timber to support the keel, the huge cranes and gantries towering above the skyline, and the stage by stage erection of the complex steel shapes within a mass of scaffolding and supports, all catch the eye and the imagination. The men working upon the creation of this new ship are dwarfed by their own achievement. And then comes the day when the ship slowly slides down the slipway to take to the water for the first time. No one can resist applauding at such a moment! Two of Sealink's ships are seen here in various stages of construction in the shipyard, in a brief pictorial tribute to the men who build the ships.

164   The ribs of the *Senlac* are taking shape, in the dry dock at the Naval Yards at Brest in France.   *Sealink UK*

165   Nearing completion, the *Senlac* is recognisable beneath the scaffolding. Soon she will be ready for launching.   *Sealink UK*

166   Spick and span, the new *Senlac* shows off her smart livery at Newhaven. *Ambrose Greenway*

164

165   166

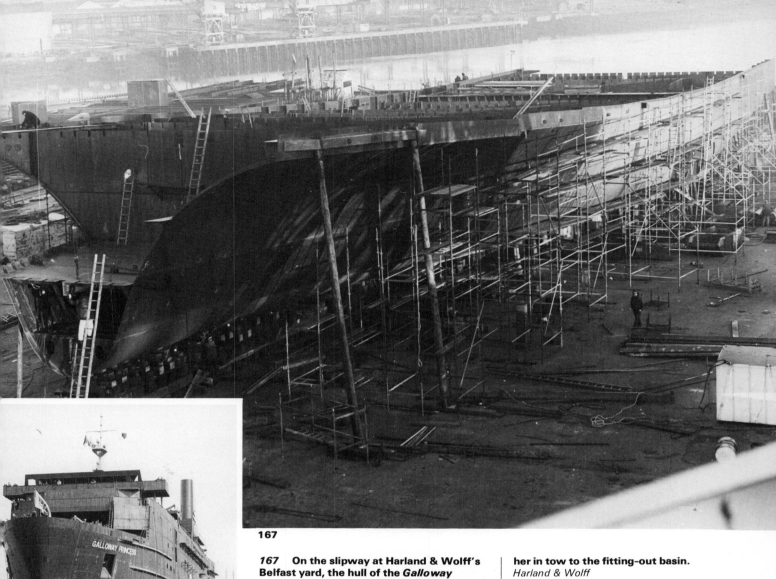

167

168

169

167 On the slipway at Harland & Wolff's Belfast yard, the hull of the *Galloway Princess* is well advanced in construction, with the keel sitting upon a massive array of wooden supports.   *Harland & Wolff*

168 The *Galloway Princess* takes to the water at the Belfast yard of Harland & Wolff. Tugs wait in the background to take her in tow to the fitting-out basin.   *Harland & Wolff*

169 After launching, the *Galloway Princess* undergoes fitting-out and final painting at Belfast, with the giant Samson crane towering above.   *Harland & Wolff*

170 The *Galloway Princess* at sea.
Sealink UK

170

8. Design for the Passenger

Today's Sealink traveller enjoys an environment which has been evolved by a consistent policy of good design, inaugurated by the then BTC in the late 1950s and continued to this day by the British Railways Board and Sealink UK Ltd. The BTC established a Design Panel, to advise them on the aesthetic and industrial design elements in their massive £1,240million modernisation programme which was announced in 1955.

The Design Panel was requested to advise generally on the policy to be followed in dealing with the design problems which were bound to arise in different fields, as the BTC launched this vast programme of new construction and modernisation of its trains, ships, and structures — a programme long overdue! In 1955 there were still many signs on British Railways of neglect and obsolescence dating from the wartime years, but successive governments had failed to finance a comprehensive scheme for rebuilding and modernisation; so a policy of 'make do and mend' had sufficed for a decade. Now, in 1955, the 'go ahead' was at last given, and the BTC was determined that the money should be

spent to the utmost advantage, and certainly not least in those areas directly affecting the passenger.

Before describing the Design Panel, and the work of its consultants, it is of some relevance to briefly take a look at the passenger amenities which were enjoyed by the travelling public on the railway ships of the immediate postwar period; a period when the 'classic' passenger and the steam-turbine 'scaled-down' liner were still the essence of the services. The ships catered for the same range of classes that the British and Continental railways offered. It was still possible to cross the Channel in the first class comfort of prewar days and make the rail journey by Pullman or Wagon-Lits sleeping car; at a price of course. For the very rich, 'de luxe' cabins (especially on the longer sea crossings) offered a quality of privacy and comfort comparable to the ocean-going liners, and many famous personages, including members of the royal families, chose to avail themselves of this mode of travel. The aeroplane has largely taken this prestige market today of course.

The general standard of amenity to be found in the postwar fleet, at the time of

nationalisation, differed but little from that existing when war was declared in 1939. It was a standard which had slowly evolved as the steamships had grown in size and technical stature over the previous 50 years or so. It may, in retrospect, be described as 'solid', as 'unimaginative but comfortable' sometimes as 'flowery', but most of the time 'basic'. For example, a first class cabin, with homely fabrics and fittings nevertheless had all the wiring and

171   The Wessex Bar in Sealink's cross-Channel ferry *Hengist* provides a striking comparison with the outdoor rigours of a Victorian steamer, as vividly portrayed in the pre-Raphaelite painting by Ford Maddox Brown entitled 'The Last of England', painted in 1855.   *Sealink UK*

172   First class single cabin on A deck of the LNER steam-turbine ship the *Arnhem*, the first postwar cross-Channel ship the LNER placed in service, in 1947. The wiring visible to the eye was an electrician's dream! *British Rail*

173   The first class smoking room on the *Falaise*, built in 1947 and designed for the SR passenger services from Southampton. *British Rail*

172

173

174   **175**

plumbing in full view; excellent no doubt for repair, but scarcely aesthetic! The lounges had the same stolid comfort that commercial hotels offered on dry land, and the decor of these lounges sometimes echoed the 'tearooms' of the 1930s; only the elderly 'string quartet' was missing. For the second and third class traveller, open decks abounded and there was no guarantee of a seat under cover. The smokerooms, bars and lounges they could use were curiously masculine in their furnishings — intended for the robust mariner rather than the frail and travel-sick, old or young!

Comfort there certainly was; at a price. Quality of service there certainly was; the ships' crews are renowned for their pride in this. What was missing was a sense of reality, a sense of the winds of change that were blowing in postwar Europe. As I have remarked in an earlier book (*British Rail, 1948-1978: A Journey By Design*, Ian Allan Ltd 1979), it is a sobering thought that the same year that saw the steam turbine ship *Maid of Orleans* (1,400 passengers but only 30 cars) placed in service, also witnessed the maiden flight of the world's first jet civil airliner, the de Havilland Comet and the following year saw the first Vickers Viscount turboprop airliner enter service on British European Airways. As the 'jet age' commenced, British Railways was still firmly ensconced in the 'steam age', on land and at sea, and even the latest ships were as already stated, conceived in prewar terms. Yet to come was the realisation of the enormity of the competitive challenge of the aeroplane and the motor car, and of how this was to change the habits and expectations of the travelling public.

Public demand largely dictates commercial requirement, and by 1952 the Southern Region were pointing a finger to the future trend, by introducing their new *Lord Warden*, the first drive-on, drive-off car ferry built for the BTC. (The LMSR introduced the *first* railway owned sea-

going stern loading car ferry, the *Princess Victoria* just prior to the war.) The *Lord Warden* was one class only, and could carry 700 passengers and 120 cars; a greatly changed ratio of people to cars. Her accommodation when new consisted of a smokeroom (quaint term!) on the boat deck, a buffet, large lounge and restaurant on the promenade deck and (shades of the past) seven two-berth passenger cabins with private toilet facilities; there was also a 'Ladies only' room. (There were still 'Ladies only' compartments on some BR trains at this time.)

A second purpose-built car ferry was ordered for the same service, to replace the elderly *Dinard*, and it was this vessel, the *Maid of Kent*, introduced in 1959 which first demonstrated the work of the Design Panel and its consultants. As I have briefly described at the beginning of this chapter, the BTC believed that in order to keep abreast of contemporary ideas in design, a large public organisation, such as itself, must make use of the services of professional designers and consultants from outside the industry, as well as of its own staff. At the commencement of the brief given for establishing the Design Panel in 1956, within the BTC management structure, the members of the commission laid down some specific design objectives for the new equipment of the Modernisation Programme, as follows:

(a) The appearance of the equipment must invest it with a character appropriate to a great public service and in keeping with the prestige of the commission.

(b) The liveliness and vitality of the appearance of the equipment must project the idea of a keen and progressive management.

(c) The attractiveness of the equipment must promote the commercial development of the commission's activities and engender pride among those who use it.

A part of the new Design Panel's job was to promote interest in design among the staff, and it was to have mainly an advisory status and only partially an executive status. In other words, if an engineer or architect chose to decline the advice of the panel's consultants, he was free to do so. However, this has rarely been the case, happily!

The BTC Design Panel first met on 8 August 1956 and 11 months later Mr George Williams joined the BTC as Design Officer and head of the executive department of the Design Panel. George Williams was a designer of some note, and had gained his early experience in the motor industry. He spent the war years in the Royal Navy, designing acoustic and magnetic aircraft-laid weapons; returning to the professional design world afterwards. He was Senior Industrial Officer at the Council of Industrial Design before joining the BTC. George Williams was well practised in the art of dealing with engineers and manufacturers who sometimes had a deep distrust of 'arty' types, and he laid the foundations for today's excellent relationship between

174 **The first class Ladies lounge on the cross-Channel turbine steamer** *Maid of Orleans*, **introduced on the Folkestone-Boulogne route in July 1949.** *British Rail*

175 **A first class de luxe cabin on the** *Maid of Orleans*; **offering considerable comfort and privacy despite the short crossing time on the English Channel.** *British Rail*

176 **A corner of the second class lounge on the ER Harwich-Hook of Holland ship the** *Amsterdam* **introduced in 1950.** *British Rail*

177 **By the time the** *Amsterdam* **appeared (sister ship to the** *Arnhem*) **in 1950, the cabin design had been refined considerably, and the layout of the electrical fittings and washstand is quite neat in this two-berth first class cabin; even if the textile designs are a trifle 'flowery'.** *British Rail*

these branches of British Rail, and of Sealink UK Ltd.

George Williams and his small but enthusiastic staff, worked tremendously hard in the first years of the modernisation plan, and locomotives, carriages, ships, uniforms, styles of lettering, liveries, furnishings — all came under review. The *Maid of Kent* (where the treatment of the public room were described by the *Guardian's* London correspondent as 'a credit to British Railways') became known as the 'Pocket Liner' because of her good looks and passenger amenities. She was the first ship to break away from the stodgy furnishings which had characterised the postwar-built railway ships, and the consultant design firm of Ward and Austin (now Ward Associates) produced a cheerful but extremely practical range of furnishings (incidentally commencing a working association with the Naval Architect of the BR ships that continues to this day).

I have given a full account of the creation and achievements of the Design Panel in *British Rail 1948-1978: A Journey by Design* (Ian Allan Ltd 1979), and here I would only wish to mention that tragically George Williams died suddenly, whilst the tangible results of his hard work were only just beginning to make a real impact upon the travelling public. His greatest achievement was the creation of the British Rail Corporate Identity programme, as already described on pages 74-77; which he never saw in its full realisation.

Today the BRB Design Panel continues to play a very important role in monitoring design standards and advising upon new equipment, uniforms, liveries and so on. The Director of Industrial Design, Mr James Cousins, and his staff report to the Design Panel at quarterly meetings. The Panel (as has been the policy since its inception) consists of a mixture of Railway's Board members and people from outside the industry. One member of today's Design Panel is Mr David Kirby, until recently Managing Director of Sealink UK Ltd and this ensures a continuing liaison now that Sealink is less directly a BRB-managed concern.

Sealink UK Ltd's Principal Naval Architect, Tony Rogan, has established a very happy and close working relationship with Ward Associates, and between them they have more than 20 ships to their credit since the *Maid of Kent*. Over this period of some 23 years or so, a consistent policy of good design has been followed, although it has had to be adaptable to changing commercial requirements and to other factors such as more stringent fire and safety regulations, as well as to the changing habits of the public.

To understand how the interior design and layout of a present-day Sealink ferry has evolved, when seen in terms of passenger comfort and amenity, it is necessary to consider briefly some of the limitations imposed upon the Naval Architect and the Industrial Designer from the outset. All the ships of Sealink are of course engineered and constructed to meet the stringent requirements of Lloyd's Register of Shipping, as well as those of the British Board of Trade construction rules for safety at sea and seaworthiness for passenger ships. They must also conform to fire protection and firefighting regulations.

Once these requirements are met, the designer can be briefed with the commercial department's requirement. This will give the route, or type of service, the ship is intended for; the number of passengers, cars, vehicles, etc; the catering facilities required; shops, cabins, lounges, staircases, entrances, and so on. The Naval Architect's department will have schemed a layout of all these amenities, bearing in mind the problems of circulation within the ship and also the problems of entering and leaving.

Another limitation upon the Naval Architect is that Sealink's ships are limited in their overall size — length, breadth and draught — by the harbours they use and

176

177

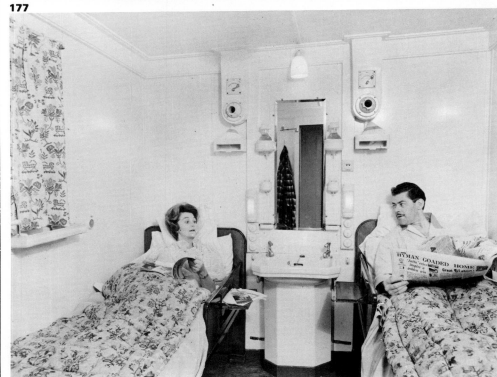

the seas they navigate. No dramatic increase in gross tonnage is therefore possible without (for example) extensive dredging in inner harbour areas, and rebuilding of quays or vehicle ramps to suit. It can be said of the latest ferries for the Stranraer-Larne and Dover-Calais routes, that these are just about as big as can be normally accommodated. Therefore any increase in passenger or vehicle capacity has to be won from clever use of the ship's interior (see previous chapter).

All Sealink's ships have to be suitable for all-the-year-round operations, sometimes under difficult weather or working conditions and with tides in awkward phases. They have to be powerful enough to keep time in adverse weather and very manoeuvrable within ports (not needing assistance from tugs). Above all, the time they spend in port is often very short, so it is necessary to guarantee ease of loading and unloading and good passenger circulation areas and staircases or lifts. This quick turnround also dictates that the ships must be easy to clean and maintain. It does not require much effort to imagine the chaos a large party of schoolchildren can wreak in mid-summer; all the litter has to be cleared and the area cleaned ready for the next sailing — sometimes only 90 minutes later!

A policy of a seat under cover for every passenger is followed and, recently, with the growth of the road haulage vehicle traffic, special amenities for lorry drivers have been provided on the four latest ships, with for example on the *St David* a self-contained lounge/restaurant. Air-conditioning, sound insulation and good intercom/loudspeaker arrangements are now the established norm for all Sealink's new ferries.

And so, presented with a brief, the Design Consultant sets about producing passenger areas (and other important staff-only areas) which are cheerful, pleasing, practical and not wildly extravagant. (He is of course set a budget to work within.) The fabrics of seating for example, must be pleasing to the eye, but easy to clean and so too the curtains and carpets, and the furnishings of sleeping berths, or cabins. Decor for the wall surfaces, for bars and catering counters, must be smart and easy to wash down. The design of chairs and tables must be robust and avoid sharp edges or projections which could cause injury in rough weather, and so on. Above all, the designer has to create a pleasing shipboard environment, where the passenger feels secure and relaxed. It is not just the peak periods with 1,000 passengers or more on board that he must consider; it is also the off-season traffic when perhaps less than 50 passengers are carried, and these usually on the darkest, bleakest days of the year! It is important to make them feel comfortable, and not feeling like 'peas in a barrel'.

Ward Associates have succeeded in creating a pleasing modern environment on Sealink's ferries. Each ship has its own individual characteristics and colours for interiors; there is no rigid standardisation for the sake of it. For one thing the ships' crews as well as many passengers like to be able to recognise which ship they are on by means of its furnishings and layout. Where standardisation is a sensible policy, for example in the layout and fittings of cabins, it has been introduced, but many areas of the ships, and in particular the lounges and restaurants have, as I have said, been given a pleasing individual identity; sometimes by the use of murals or other pictorial devices.

The tastes of the traveller change, and Sealink closely watches these trends and keeps a policy of awareness and modification up its sleeve! For example, not so long ago the idea of discotheques on board ship on the longer routes to provide entertainment for the younger travellers, seemed a good marketing advantage, and these were included in the layout of some new ferries. However, today the cinema is back in vogue, and the former 'discos' are now 'mini-cinemas' in

178

179

some cases! Also, there was a period when self-service shops were seen as the best way to cater for the stream of duty-free customers; here again, personal staff counter service has replaced it.

Catering is a particularly good barometer of public attitudes and finances. The 1960s saw a strong trend away from restaurants in favour of cafeterias and self-service and a number of ships had their catering facilities altered to meet this demand. The 'buffet' and the 'snack' were more popular than the waiter-served meal at the table. However, the traditional restaurant has survived all this, and on the longer sea routes in particular it remains popular because it offers the passenger not only an excellent menu, but the ability to relax in comfortable surroundings. Today's general Sealink policy is a sensible one, of catering for both the 'snack' and the more complete meal.

The latest Sealink ferries, the *Galloway Princess*, *St Anselm*, *St Christopher* and *St David* have all the main passenger areas and amenities grouped on the one deck, except for the tea bar and tea lounge (or in the case of the *St David* the bar) which are above the promenade deck, and with this internal layout the designer has provided a simplified basic grouping of areas. No longer can the passenger quickly become so disorientated that within five minutes of boarding the ship he or she does not remember which end, or which deck, they are on! (And this,

180

despite excellent graphic signposting.) The one-deck layout, with transverse arrangement for the lounges, shops, etc, is a definite advance in terms of passenger comfort.

The work of the Naval Architect and the Industrial Designer has made an important contribution towards creating an efficient modern image for sea travel. The ferries offer an environment equal to, or perhaps even better than, their airborne counterparts, and today's passenger — with or without road vehicle — is well provided for.

178 Quite a degree of comfort for the short crossing to the Isle of Wight, but the furnishings are curiously dated in concept. The motor vessel *Shanklin's* after saloon is illustrated. Note the chain holding the table to the floor (lower left of picture). The *Shanklin* was introduced into service in 1951. *British Rail*

179 The first class smoke room on the *Normannia* introduced in 1952, for the SR's Southampton-Le Havre service. Ponderous in the extreme! *British Rail*

180 The *Lord Warden's* shop. This car ferry (1952) with one-class accommodation was the first real move by the BTC towards adapting its ships to a changed clientele. Gone were the prewar 'classic' passengers seeking the privacy of a cabin or willing to pay for first class services. Now the motorist and family, holiday-bound and in search of duty-free gifts and purchases was a rapidly developing market. *Sealink UK*

181 Side lounge on the *Maid of Kent*, introduced in 1959. This one class passenger and vehicle ferry was the first ship to receive the attentions of the BTC Design Panel and its consultants. It was custom-built for the new generation of travellers and their cars. The policy was 'a seat for everyone, under cover'. Gone were the draughty gangways and smoky lounges and the alternatives of stiff sea breezes or fuggy interiors. The *Maid of Kent* brought a new look to the cross-Channel fleet. *British Rail*

181

182

183

184

182 The smoke room of the turbine steamship *Caledonian Princess*, introduced in 1961 for the Stranraer-Larne car ferry service. 400 first class and 1,000 second class passengers were accommodated. *British Rail*

183 By the time the car ferry *Dover* entered service in 1965, the style and quality of the railway ships' interiors had been transformed. A comparison with, for example, the *Normannia* photograph 179 shows this well. This is a view of a portion of the smoke room bar on the *Dover*. *Ward Associates*

184 The second class forward lounge on the *St George*, a two-class passenger and vehicle ferry for the Harwich-Hook of Holland service, introduced 1968. *British Rail*

185 The first class restaurant and tea lounge on the *St George*; for comparison the original designer's perspective drawing for this area is shown. *British Rail*

186 The bar of the Isle of Wight ferry *Cuthred*, a one-class ferry on the Portsmouth/Lymington-Isle of Wight service; introduced in 1969. *Ward Associates*

185

186

187

187 A portion of the cafeteria on the multi-purpose one-class ferry, the *Vortigern*, introduced on the Dover-Dunkerque service in 1969. *British Rail*

188 The Britannia Bar, of multi-purpose ferry *Vortigern*. *Ward Associates*

189 Stairway on the *Hengist*, 1972, with decorative fibreglass semi-relief mural. *British Rail*

190 The restaurant on the one-class passenger and vehicle ferry *Hengist*. *British Rail*

191 The cafeteria on both the *Hengist* and *Horsa* feature decorative etched glass panels. *Ward Associates*

188

189

190

191

192

193

194

192 The second class central lounges on the *St Edmund*, looking aft. *Ward Associates*

193 Second class bar on the two-class Harwich-Hook of Holland ferry, the *St Edmund*; introduced in 1974. *Ward Associates*

194 The first class restaurant on the *St Edmund*. *Ward Associates*

195 Part of the first class bar on the *St Columba*, introduced on the Holyhead-Dun Laoghaire service in 1977. *Ward Associates*

196 The first class portside lounge (a view of part) of the *St Columba*. *Ward Associates*

197 The second class starboard lounge on the *St Columba*. *Ward Associates*

195

196

197

198

199

200

201

202

203

204

204 The midships lounge in *St Anselm*.
Ward Associates

205 *St Anselm's* tea bar. *Ward Associates*

206 The duty-free counter in the lounge
of the *St Anselm*, seen in 1981. *British Rail*

205

206

Pictorial Interlude : In Coats of many Colours

When the sad day comes for a ship of the Sealink fleet, and she makes her last sailing, it marks the end of her usefulness, but it does not always signify the end of a career. Some ships are sold to the shipbreakers, but others find buyers from elsewhere in the world. These new owners often modify the architecture of the ship to suit different services, and of course the once-familiar Sealink livery is replaced by coats of many colours. A few ex-Sealink ships are pictured here in their new guises, and in new surroundings; captured by the camera of Ambrose Greenway.

207

208
209

207 The Chandris cruise ship *Fiorita* glides into Corfu on a calm autumn morning in 1977. Formerly Sealink's *Amsterdam* of the Harwich-Hook overnight service, she was sold in 1970 and has mainly been employed on seven-day cruises from Venice to the Aegean, interspersed with periods of lay up and a short spell as an accommodation ship for oil rig constructors at Stord in Norway. *Ambrose Greenway*

208 Another Chandris cruise ship the *Radiosa* leaving Mykonos for Porto Rafi on the Greek mainland. Licensed to carry 735 deck passengers on day trips she is barely recognisable as the former Southern Railway's 12 passenger cargo vessel *Winchester*, once well known on the Channel Islands run. *Ambrose Greenway*

209 The distinctive 'cabs' on the bridge wings of *Athens Express* betray her former incarnation as Belgium's first purpose built car ferry *Prinses Josephine Charlotte*. Renamed *Leto* following her sale in 1976 she adopted her present name before entering service on the Piraeus-Rhodes run. *Ambrose Greenway*

210   Looking little different from her days
as SNCF's *Lisieux* on the Newhaven–Dieppe
service the *Apollon* leaves Mykonos in
September 1977 for her daily return trip to
Piraeus. She served Greek owners
P. Nomikos and latterly Agapitos Bros on
this route from 1966 until September 1980
when boiler trouble forced her withdrawal
to a lay up berth at Perama.
Ambrose Greenway

211   The former *Duke of Argyll*, the only
one of the 1956-built trio for the Heysham–
Belfast route to remain in service, seen at
Patras in her present guise as Libra
Maritime's *Neptunia*. In her smart new
livery of red and black funnel and light grey
hull she maintains a regular service
between Ancona, Piraeus and Haifa, with
intermediate calls at Corfu and Rhodes.
Ambrose Greenway

212   The Channel Islands mail ship *Sarnia*
was sold in 1978 to become the red-hulled
Aquamart, pictured here in the West India
Dock following her abortive attempt to run
duty free shopping trips between Ostend
and Dunkerque. Early in 1979 she was
towed to Greece as *Golden Star* of Grecian
Fertility Inc but has yet to see further
service, though recent photographs show
her in all white livery with a new stern
door.   *Ambrose Greenway*

210

211

212

9. The Sealink Fleet List

213

213 Earl William, with attendant gulls.
Ambrose Greenway

This pictorial section provides a list of the full Sealink fleet, as at the end of September 1981, and the routes the vessels were operating on including ships carrying the Sealink brand name but owned by the constituent companies. In addition to this list of Sealink UK Ltd ships it must be mentioned that the company owns other miscellaneous craft such as tugs and dredgers; two are described. The practice today is to switch a ship from one route to another to meet peak demands, or to cover for an emergency due to non-availability. Therefore it is possible that the routes attributed to the ships listed may have changed by the time this book is published, in one or two instances. It is also possible some older ships will have been withdrawn for scrap, or sale for use elsewhere.

The following abbreviations are used: **MV:** Motor vessel, **SS:** Steamship, **GRT:** Gross registered tonnage, **NRT:** Net registered tonnage, **RHV:** Road haulage vehicle. Measurements are metric unless specifically stated otherwise. Speed shown is service speed in Knots.

Sea Routes: European
1. Harwich-Hook of Holland

214 MV St George. Ambrose Greenway
Type: Passenger and vehicle ferry
Speed: 21kts
Built: 1968
GRT: 7,356
NRT: 3,868
Length (oa): 128m
Breadth (oa): 20.57m
Draught (loaded): 5.03m
Passengers: 1,200
Cars: 220
Freight: —
RHV space: 210 (linear metres)

215 MV St Edmund. Ambrose Greenway
Type: Passenger and vehicle ferry
Speed: 21kts
Built: 1974
GRT: 8,987
NRT: 3,868
Length (oa): 131.6m
Breadth (oa): 22.6m
Draught (loaded): 5.18m
Passengers: 1,400
Cars: 296
Freight: —
RHV space: 387 (linear metres)

216 MV Koningin Juliana **owned by Zeeland Steamship Co.** *Ambrose Greenway*
Type: Passenger and vehicle ferry
Speed: 21kts
Built: 1968
GRT: 6,682
NRT: 3,475
Length (oa): 131.20m
Breadth (oa): 20.46m
Draught (loaded): 5.18m
Passengers: 1,200
Cars: 220
Freight: —
RHV space: 210 (linear metres)

217 MV Prinses Beatrix **owned by Zeeland Steamship Co.** *Ambrose Greenway*
Type: Passenger and vehicle ferry
Speed: 21kts
Built: 1978
GRT: 9,238
NRT: 5,064
Length (oa): 131.9m
Breadth (oa): 23.5m
Draught (loaded): 5.18m
Passengers: 1,500
Cars: 320
Freight: —
RHV space: 582 (linear metres)

214

215

216
218

217

2. Harwich–Zeebrugge (container)

218   MV Sea Freightliner. *Sealink UK*
Type: Container ship
Speed: 13.5kts
Built: 1968
GRT: 4,034
NRT: 2,108
Length (oa): 118.26m
Breadth (oa): 16.76m
Draught (loaded): 4.42m
Passengers: —
Cars: —
Freight: 3,000ton
RHV space: —

219   MV Sea Freightliner II.
Ambrose Greenway
Type: Container ship
Speed: 13.5kts
Built: 1968
GRT: 4,034
NRT: 2,108
Length (oa): 118.26m
Breadth (oa): 16.76m
Draught (loaded): 4.42m
Passengers: —
Cars: —
Freight: 3,000ton
RHV space: —

220   MV Brathay Fisher.
Ambrose Greenway
Type: Container ship
Speed: 14.5kts
Built: 1971
GRT: 3,604
NRT: 1,031
Length (oa): 105.92m
Breadth (oa): 16.79m
Draught (loaded): 5.50m
Passengers: —
Cars: —
Freight: 2,476ton
RHV space: —

219

220

221

223

222
224

3. Harwich–Zeebrugge/ Dunkerque (Train Ferry)

221   MV Essex Ferry. *British Rail*
Type: Train ferry and container ship
Speed: 13.5kts
Built: 1957
GRT: 3,089
NRT: 1,477
Length (oa): 122m
Breadth (oa): 18.59m
Draught (loaded): 3.69m
Passengers: —
Cars: —
Freight: 1,770ton
RHV space: 351 (linear metres)

222   MV Norfolk Ferry.
Ambrose Greenway
Type: Train ferry and container ship
Speed: 13.5kts
Built: 1951
GRT: 3,157
NRT: 1,408
Length (oa): 121.62m
Breadth (oa): 18.59m
Draught (loaded): 3.69m
Passengers: —
Cars: —
Freight: 1,770ton
RHV space: 351 (linear metres)

223   MV Cambridge Ferry.
Ian Allan Library
Type: Train ferry and container ship
Speed: 13.5kts
Built: 1963
GRT: 3,294
NRT: 1,111
Length (oa): 122.83m
Breadth (oa): 18.59m
Draught (loaded): 3.43m
Passengers: —
Cars: —
Freight: 879ton
RHV space: 354 (linear metres)

224   MV Speedlink Vanguard. *Sealink UK*
Type: Train ferry and cargo ship
Speed: 17kts
Built: 1973
GRT: 2,514
NRT: 1,245
Length (oa): 142.30m
Breadth (oa): 16.41m
Draught (loaded): 5.92
Passengers: 12
Cars: —
Freight (capacity): 53 wagons
RHV space: —

4. Dover–Dunkerque

225 MV Vortigern. *British Rail*
Type: Multi-purpose/passenger/vehicle/train
Speed: 19.5kts
Built: 1969
GRT: 4,371
NRT: 1,594
Length (oa): 114.57m
Breadth (oa): 19.2m
Draught (loaded): 4.08m
Passengers: 1,000
Cars: 240
Freight: 840ton
RHV space: 366 (linear metres)

**226 MV Saint Germain owned by SNCF;
flies French flag.** *Ambrose Greenway*
Type: Multi-purpose/train/container/passenger
Speed: 18.5kts
Built: 1951
GRT: 3,492
NRT: 1,276
Length (oa): 115.7m
Breadth (oa): 18.4m
Draught (loaded): 4.11m
Passengers: 1,000
Cars: 135
Freight: —
RHV space: 350 (linear metres)

**227 MV Saint Eloi owned by Angleterre-
Lorraine-Alsace Co ALA.**
Ambrose Greenway
Type: Multi-purpose/train/container/passenger
Speed: 19.5kts
Built: 1974
GRT: 4,469
NRT: 1,849
Length (oa): 114.60m
Breadth (oa): 19.2m
Draught (loaded): 4.11m
Passengers: 1,000
Cars: 160
Freight: —
RHV space: 366 (linear metres)

225

226

227

228
230

229

5. Dover/Folkestone–Ostend

All vessels on this service are owned by RTM

228 MV Koningin Fabiola.
Ambrose Greenway
Type: Passenger and vehicle ferry
Speed: 22kts
Built: 1962
GRT: 3,745
NRT: 1,777
Length (oa): 116.55m
Breadth (oa): 15.97m
Draught (loaded): 3.82m
Passengers: 1,200
Cars: 88
Freight: —
RHV space: 76 (linear metres)

229 MV Prins Phillippe.
Ambrose Greenway
Type: Passenger and vehicle ferry
Speed: 22kts
Built: 1973
GRT: 5,000
NRT: 2,008
Length (oa): 118.4m
Breadth (oa): 19.8m
Draught (loaded): 4.25m
Passengers: 1,302
Cars: 212
Freight: —
RHV space: 174 (linear metres)

The Sealink Fleet List

230   MV Prins Laurent.
Ambrose Greenway
Type: Passenger and vehicle ferry
Speed: 22kts
Built: 1974
GRT: 4,909
NRT: 1,987
Length (oa): 118.4m
Breadth (oa): 19.8m
Draught (loaded): 4.25m
Passengers: 1,302
Cars: 170
Freight: —
RHV space: 380 (linear metres)

231   MV Princesse Astrid.
Ambrose Greenway
Type: Passenger and vehicle ferry
Speed: 22kts
Built: 1968
GRT: 3,148
NRT: 1,267
Length (oa): 117.2m
Breadth (oa): 16m
Draught (loaded): 3.80m
Passengers: 850
Cars: 160
Freight: —
RHV space: 95 (linear metres)

232   MV Prinses Paola.
Ambrose Greenway
Type: Passenger ship
Speed: 24kts
Built: 1966
GRT: 4,356
NRT: 2,084
Length (oa): 116.77m
Breadth (oa): 16m
Draught (loaded): 3,8m
Passengers: 1,700
Cars: —
Freight: —
RHV space: —

233   MV Reine Astrid.   *Ambrose Greenway*
Type: Passenger ship
Speed: 24kts
Built: 1958
GRT: 3,389
NRT: 1,510
Length (oa): 113.9m
Breadth (oa): 14.88m
Draught (loaded): 3.94m
Passengers: 1,700
Cars: —
Freight: —
RHV space: —

234   MV Roi Baudouin.   *British Rail*
Type: Passenger and vehicle ferry
Speed: 22kts
Built: 1965
GRT: 3,241
NRT: 1,432
Length (oa): 117m
Breadth (oa): 16m
Draught (loaded): 3.8m
Passengers: 850
Cars: 160
Freight: —
RHV space: 95 (linear metres)

235   MV Prinses Maria Esmeralda.
Ambrose Greenway
Type: Passenger and vehicle ferry
Speed: 22kts
Built: 1975
GRT: 5,543
NRT: 2,471
Length (oa): 118.4m
Breadth (oa): 20.7m
Draught (loaded): 4.52m
Passengers: 1,200
Cars: 300
Freight: —
RHV space: 450 (linear metres)

231

232

233

236   MV Princesse Marie Christine.
Ambrose Greenway
Type: Passenger and vehicle ferry
Speed: 22kts
Built: 1976
GRT: 5,543
NRT: 2,471
Length (oa): 118.4m
Breadth (oa): 20.7m
Draught (loaded): 4.52m
Passengers: 1,200
Cars: 300
Freight: —
RHV space: 450 (linear metres)

237   MV Prins Albert.   *Ambrose Greenway*
Type: Passenger and vehicle ferry
Speed: 22kts
Built: 1978
GRT: 6,019
NRT: 2,701
Length (oa): 118.4m
Breadth (oa): 20.7m
Draught (loaded): 4.52
Passengers: 1,400
Cars: 250
Freight: —
RHV space: 427 (linear metres)

234

235

236

237

6. Dover/Folkestone–Calais/Boulogne

238   MV Hengist. *Ambrose Greenway*
Type: Passenger and vehicle ferry
Speed: 19.5kts
Built: 1972
GRT: 5,590
NRT: 2,008
Length (oa): 117.5m
Breadth (oa): 19.81m
Draught (loaded): 3.96m
Passengers: 1,400
Cars: 217
Freight: —
RHV space: 366 (linear metres)

239   MV Horsa. *Richard Capper*
Type: Passenger and vehicle ferry
Speed: 19.5kts
Built: 1972
GRT: 5,590
NRT: 2,008
Length (oa): 117.5m
Breadth (oa): 19.81m
Draught (loaded): 3.96m
Passengers: 1,400
Cars: 217
Freight: —
RHV space: 366 (linear metres)

240   MV Chantilly owned by the SNCF.
SNCF.
Type: Passenger and vehicle ferry
Speed: 19.5kts
Built: 1966
GRT: 3,400
NRT: 873
Length (oa): 109.9m
Breadth (oa): 18.54m
Draught (loaded): 4.2m
Passengers: 1,350
Cars: 160
Freight: —
RHV space: 320 (linear metres)

241   MV Chartres owned by the SNCF.
Ambrose Greenway
Type: Passenger and vehicle ferry
Speed: 20.5kts
Built: 1974
GRT: 4,586
NRT: 1,648
Length (oa): 115.4m
Breadth (oa): 19.2m
Draught (loaded): 4.2m
Passengers: 1,400
Cars: 250
Freight: —
RHV space: 350 (linear metres)

242   MV Anderida sold to Covenant Shipping Inc, Monrovia, Liberia on 30 October 1981. *Ambrose Greenway*
Type: Vehicle ferry
Speed: 17kts
Built: 1972
GRT: 1,579
NRT: 565
Length (oa): 108.2m
Breadth (oa): 16.46m
Draught (loaded): 4m
Passengers: 36
Cars: —
Freight: 760ton
RHV space: 560 (linear metres)

243   MV St Anselm. *ISR*
Type: Multi-purpose ferry
Speed: 19.5kts
Built: 1980
GRT: 7,003
NRT: 3,386
Length (oa): 129.4m
Breadth (oa): 21.6m
Draught (loaded): 5.01m
Passengers: 1,000
Cars: 309
Freight: —
RHV space: 780 (linear metres)

238

239

240

241

242

243

The Sealink Fleet List

244   MV St Christopher.
Type: Multi-purpose ferry
Speed: 19.5kts
Built: 1981
GRT: 7,003
NRT: 3,386
Length (oa): 129.4m
Breadth (oa): 21.6m
Draught (loaded): 5.01m
Passengers: 1,000
Cars: 309
Freight: —
RHV space: 780 (linear metres)

245   MV Côte d'Azur owned by the SNCF.
Type: Multi-purpose ferry
Speed: 20kts
Built: 1981
GRT: —
NRT: —
Length (oa): 130m
Breadth (oa): 12.5m
Draught (loaded): —
Passengers: 1,400
Cars: 330
Freight: —
RHV space: 54×15m lorries

244

245

246

247
249

248

7. Newhaven–Dieppe

Joint service with SNCF

246   MV Senlac. *British Rail*
Type: Passenger and vehicle ferry
Speed: 19.5kts
Built: 1973
GRT: 5,590
NRT: 2,016
Length (oa): 117.5m
Breadth (oa): 19.8m
Draught (loaded): 4.11m
Passengers: 1,400
Cars: 217
Freight: —
RHV space: 366 (linear metres)

247   MV Villandry flies the French flag.
Ambrose Greenway
Type: Passenger and vehicle ferry
Speed: 19kts
Built: 1965
GRT: 3,628
NRT: 973
Length (oa): 105m
Breadth (oa): 17.57m
Draught (loaded): 3.95m
Passengers: 1,200
Cars: 160
Freight: —
RHV space: 310 (linear metres)

248   MV Valencay flies the French flag.
British Rail
Type: Passenger and vehicle ferry
Speed: 19kts
Built: 1965
GRT: 3,430
NRT: 977
Length (oa): 104.9m
Breadth (oa): 17.1m
Draught (loaded): 3.96m
Passengers: 1,200
Cars: 160
Freight: —
RHV space: 152 (linear metres)

8. Weymouth–Cherbourg

249   The turbine steamer *Maid of Kent* (see page 44) was withdrawn at the end of the season. The 1982 season is likely to see this service worked by the *Ailsa Princess*.
British Rail

250

251

9. Holyhead-Dun Laoghaire

250   MV St Columba. *Sealink UK*
Type: Passenger and vehicle ferry
Speed: 19.5kts
Built: 1977
GRT: 7,836
NRT: 3,790
Length (oa): 129.2m
Breadth (oa): 21.2m
Draught (loaded): 4.66m
Passengers: 2,400
Cars: 334
Freight: —
RHV space: 434 (linear metres)

251   MV St David. *ISR*
Type: Multi-purpose ferry
Speed: 19.5kts
Built: 1981
GRT: 7,110
NRT: 3,487
Length (oa): 129.4m
Breadth (oa): 21.6m
Draught (loaded): 5m
Passengers: 1,000
Cars: 309
Freight: —
RHV space: 62×12m lorries

10. Holyhead-Belfast/Dublin (Container)

252   MV Brian Boroime.
Ambrose Greenway
Type: Container ship
Speed: 14.5kts
Built: 1970
GRT: 4,098
NRT: 1,882
Length (oa): 107.28m
Breadth (oa): 17.37m
Draught (loaded): 4.11m
Passengers: —
Cars: —
Freight: 2,476ton
RHV space: —

253   MV Rhodri Mawr. *Ambrose Greenway*
Type: Container ship
Speed: 14.5kts
Built: 1970
GRT: 4,095
NRT: 1,883
Length (oa): 106.98m
Breadth (oa): 17.37m
Draught (loaded): 4.11m
Passengers: —
Cars: —
Freight: 2,476ton
RHV space: —

11. Fishguard-Rosslare

Fishguard & Rosslare Railway & Harbours Company

254   MV Stena Normandica on charter.
Sealink UK
Type: Passenger and vehicle ferry
Speed: 17.5kts
Built: 1974
GRT: 5,443
NRT: 2,774
Length (oa): 120.78m
Breadth (oa): 19.51m
Draught (loaded): 5.25m
Passengers: 1,200
Cars: 470
Freight: —
RHV space: —

252

253
254

12. Stranraer-Larne

255 MV Galloway Princess. *Harland & Wolff*
Type: Multi-purpose ferry
Speed: 18.5kts
Built: 1979
GRT: 6,268
NRT: 2,675
Length (oa): 129.4m
Breadth (oa): 21.6m
Draught (loaded): 4.57m
Passengers: 1,000
Cars: 309
Freight: —
RHV space: 744 (linear metres)

256   MV Antrim Princess.
Ambrose Greenway
Type: Passenger and vehicle ferry
Speed: 19.5kts
Built: 1967
GRT: 3,630
NRT: 1,309
Length (oa): 112.47m
Breadth (oa): 17.37m
Draught (loaded): 3.65m
Passengers: 1,200
Cars: 155
Freight: 593ton
RHV space: 348 (linear metres)

257   MV Ailsa Princess. *Sealink UK*
Type: Passenger and vehicle ferry
Speed: 19.5kts
Built: 1971
GRT: 3,715
NRT: 1,279
Length (oa): 112.47m
Breadth (oa): 17.37m
Draught (loaded): 3.72m
Passengers: 1,200
Cars: 200
Freight: 600ton
RHV space: 326 (linear metres)

255

256

257

258

259

260

261

258 **MV Ulidia.** Charter terminated on 30 October 1981 and *MV Ulidia* was sold by the owners to Covenant Shipping Inc, Monrovia, Liberia. *Sealink UK*
Type: Vehicle ferry
Speed: 17kts
Built: 1970
GRT: 1,599
NRT: 633
Length (oa): 106.8m
Breadth (oa): 16.46m
Draught (loaded): 3.66m
Passengers: 36
Cars: 164
Freight: —
RHV space: 500 (linear metres)

259 **MV Darnia.** *Sealink UK*
Type: Vehicle ferry
Speed: 17.5kts
Built: 1977
GRT: 2,800
NRT: 977
Length (oa): 114.4m
Breadth (oa): 18.1m
Draught (loaded): 5.7m
Passengers: 75
Cars: —
Freight: —
RHV space: 915 (linear metres)

13. Weymouth-Channel Islands

260 **MV Earl Godwin.** *Graham B. Wise*
Type: Passenger and vehicle ferry
Speed: 19kts
Built: 1966
GRT: 4,018
NRT: 1,611
Length (oa): 99.18m
Breadth (oa): 18.38m
Draught (loaded): 4.40m
Passengers: 1,000
Cars: 185
Freight: —
RHV space: 165 (linear metres)

261 **MV Earl William.** *A. M. S. Russell*
Type: Passenger and vehicle ferry
Speed: 18kts
Built: 1964
GRT: 3,670
NRT: 1,784
Length (oa): 99.49m
Breadth (oa): 17.7m
Draught (loaded): 4.42m
Passengers: 1,000
Cars: 180
Freight: —
RHV space: 260 (linear metres)

14. Portsmouth–Channel Islands

262 MV Earl Granville. *British Rail*
Type: Passenger and vehicle ferry
Speed: 19kts
Built: 1973
GRT: 4,478
NRT: 1,982
Length (oa): 109.84m
Breadth (oa): 17.56m
Draught (loaded): 4.8m
Passengers: 1,200
Cars: 233
Freight: —
RHV space: 360 (linear metres)

262

15. Heysham–Douglas (Isle of Man)

263 MV Manx Viking. *Sealink UK*
Type: Passenger and vehicle ferry
Speed: 18kts
Built: 1976
GRT: 2,753
NRT: 1,271
Length (oa): 101.66m
Breadth (oa): 16.8m
Draught (loaded): 5m
Passengers: 800
Cars: 225
Freight: —
RHV space: —

263

264

265

16. Portsmouth/Lymington–Isle of Wight

264 MV Brading. *Ambrose Greenway*
Type: Passenger ship
Speed: 12kts
Built: 1948
GRT: 986
NRT: 530
Length (oa): 60.96m
Breadth (oa): 14.63m
Draught (loaded): 2.13m
Passengers: 1,331
Cars: —
Freight: —
RHV space: —

265 MV Southsea. *British Rail*
Type: Passenger ship
Speed: 12kts
Built: 1948
GRT: 986
NRT: 530
Length (oa): 60.96m
Breadth (oa): 14.63m
Draught (loaded): 2.13m
Passengers: 1.331
Cars: —
Freight: —
RHV space: —

266

267

268

269   **270**

271

272   **273**

266   MV Freshwater.   Ambrose Greenway
Type: Passenger and vehicle ferry
Speed: 9kts
Built: 1959
GRT: 363
NRT: 146
Length (oa): 50m
Breadth (oa): 13.11m
Draught (loaded): 1.83m
Passengers: 620
Cars: 26
Freight: —
RHV space: 68 (linear metres)

267   MV Fishbourne.   Ambrose Greenway
Type: Vehicle ferry
Speed: 9kts
Built: 1961
GRT: 293
NRT: 117
Length (oa): 50.5m
Breadth (oa): 13.11m
Draught (loaded): 1.98m
Passengers: 175
Cars: 36
Freight: —
RHV space: 74 (linear metres)

268   MV Camber Queen.
Ambrose Greenway
Type: Vehicle ferry
Speed: 9kts
Built: 1961
GRT: 293
NRT: 117

Length (oa): 50.6m
Breadth (oa): 13.11m
Draught (loaded): 1.83m
Passengers: 175
Cars: 36
Freight: —
RHV space: 74 (linear metres)

269   MV Cuthred.   Ambrose Greenway
Type: Passenger and vehicle ferry
Speed: 9kts
Built: 1969
GRT: 704
NRT: 357
Length (oa): 57.91m
Breadth (oa): 15.54m
Draught (loaded): 1.96m
Passengers: 400
Cars: 48
Freight: —
RHV space: 136 (linear metres)

270   MV Caedmon.   Ambrose Greenway
Type: Passenger and vehicle ferry
Speed: 9kts
Built: 1973
GRT: 764
NRT: 404
Length (oa): 57.91m
Breadth (oa): 15.69m
Draught (loaded): 2.28m
Passengers: 756
Cars: 76
Freight: —
RHV space: 142 (linear metres)

271   MV Cenwulf.   Ambrose Greenway
Type: Passenger and vehicle ferry
Speed: 9kts
Built: 1973
GRT: 761
NRT: 402
Length (oa): 57.91m
Breadth (oa): 15.69m
Draught (loaded): 2.28m
Passengers: 756
Cars: 76
Freight: —
RHV space: 142 (linear metres)

272   MV Cenred.   British Rail
Type: Passenger and vehicle ferry
Speed: 9kts
Built: 1973
GRT: 760
NRT: 400
Length (oa): 57.91m
Breadth (oa): 15.69m
Draught (loaded): 2.28m
Passengers: 756
Cars: 76
Freight: —
RHV space: 142 (linear metres)

17. Tilbury–Gravesend (Ferry)

273   MV Catherine.   J. G. Glover
Type: Passenger ferry
Speed: 9.25kts
Built: 1961
GRT: 214
NRT: 131
Length (oa): 33.52m
Breadth (oa): 8.53m
Draught (loaded): 1.37m
Passengers: 475
Cars: —
Freight: —
RHV space: —

274   MV Edith.   Les Bertram
Type: Passenger ferry
Speed: 9.25kts
Built: 1961
GRT: 214
NRT: 131
Length (oa): 3.52m
Breadth (oa): 8.53m
Draught (loaded): 1.37m
Passengers: 475
Cars: —
Freight: —
RHV space: —

274

18. Lake Windermere

275   MV Swan. *British Rail*
Type: Passenger ship
Speed: 11kts
Built: 1938
GRT: 251
NRT: 166
Length (oa): 42.98m
Breadth (oa): 7.92m
Draught (loaded): 1.45m
Passengers: 616
Cars: —
Freight: —
RHV space: —

276   MV Swift. *Sealink UK*
Type: Passenger ship
Speed: 11kts
Built: 1900
GRT: 203
NRT: 138
Length (oa): 48.16m
Breadth (oa): 6.40m
Draught (loaded): 1.45m
Passengers: 724
Cars: —
Freight: —
RHV space: —

277   MV Teal. *British Rail*
Type: Passenger ship
Speed: 11kts
Built: 1936
GRT: 251
NRT: 166
Length (oa): 42.98m
Breadth (oa): 7.92m
Draught (loaded): 1.45m
Passengers: 612
Cars: —
Freight: —
RHV space: —

278   MV Tern. *Sealink UK*
Type: Passenger ship
Speed: 11kts
Built: 1891
GRT: 120
NRT: 64
Length (oa): 44.2m
Breadth (oa): 5.79m
Draught (loaded): 1.37m
Passengers: 608
Cars: —
Freight: —
RHV space: —

275

276

277

278

Last — but by no means least!

279   Two very special Sealink vessels, are illustrated, as a finale to the fleet list. The *Landguard* is Sealink's only dredger, and is normally based at Harwich but has visited other ports as far apart as Stranraer, Holyhead, Weymouth and St Helier Harbour Jersey, to undertake harbour dredging. This 674ton vessel can take on board 1,000 tons of clay. *British Rail*

280   Sealink's tug, the *Meeching* is based at Newhaven where she is normally kept busy towing spoil barges and helping visiting ships to berth. From time to time a more dramatic role is played, when the *Meeching* goes to the rescue of a ship in distress, and for such occasions the crew of this sturdy little tug are on 24–hour alert. *British Rail*

279

280

Acknowledgements

In the preparation of this book I have had the constant and willing assistance of a great many people, to all of whom, my sincere thanks. The original idea was fostered by David McKenna of the British Railways Board, together with James Cousins, the Director of Industrial Design BRB, and David Kirby, then Managing Director of Sealink UK Ltd. To Messrs Jim Hannah, T. Eveleigh and A. Root, and many others in the Public Affairs and Press Offices of Sealink UK Ltd, I am also deeply indebted. My publisher, Ian Allan, and his librarian, A. B. MacLeod, have been of sympathetic assistance throughout. My sincere thanks must also go to Neville Ward and his staff, of Ward Associates, and to Messrs Harland & Wolff of Belfast. Within Sealink UK Ltd many officers have put their time at my disposal in order to explain particular facets of their daily operations and it would be invidious to single out names. In France, M Michael Bailly of the Armement Naval SNCF and his staff have also been most helpful, also Peter Mills of French Railways Ltd, London. On board ship I have had the most courteous and informative discussions with many masters and their crews, and here also it would be invidious to single out names — to *all* my sincere thanks. Without these 'on the spot' interviews (on one occasion at least in the roughest Irish Seas I have ever encountered) I could not have obtained a truly realistic picture of what Sealink is all about.

Finally, and certainly not least, I am extremely grateful to the friendly interest shown to me by a number of private individuals, all of whom share a love of the sea and of the ships described in this book. Foremost, to Ambrose Greenway who has supplied some marvellous pictures and much encouragement and to A. M. S. Russell and to M. Tetreau; two staunch enthusiasts.

To Mrs Sally Barratt a special word of thanks for much assistance and encouragement during the initial research stage.

The Author duly acknowledges the original source, or author of the various quotations contained in the narrative. He also wishes to acknowledge the considerable amount of information obtained from *Sealink News*; the house journal of Sealink UK Ltd.

281 The *Normannia*, berthed at **Newhaven.** *Ambrose Greenway*

Bibliography

Reference was made to the following books and periodicals whilst compiling this pictorial review, and the reader seeking more detailed information or historical data is recommended to them:

Brown, Ashley; *Dunkirk and the Great Western*; GWR.

Bucknall, Rixon; *Boat Trains and Channel Packets*; Vincent Stuart Ltd.

Clegg, W. P. & Styring, J. S; *British Railways Shipping and Allied Fleets*; David & Charles.

Duckworth, C. L. D. & Longmuir, G. E.; *Railway & Other Steamers*; Shipping Histories Ltd.

Greenway, Ambrose; *A Century of Cross-Channel Passenger Ferries*; Ian Allan Ltd.

Lorin, P. & Retailleau, J.; *Ships and their Secrets*; Sealink UK Ltd.

O'Mahoney, B. M. E.; *Newhaven-Dieppe 1825-1980*; Published by the Author.

Paye, P.; *The Lymington Branch*; The Oakwood Press.

The Wonder Book of Ships; Ward, Lock & Co.

Periodicals:
La Vie du Rail
Modern Railways
Sea Breezes
Sealink News
Transport Review